BOYS

Will Puberty Last my Whole Life?

REAL Answers to REAL Questions from Preteens About Body Changes, Sex, and Other Growing-Up Stuff

. . . .

Julie Metzger, RN, MN, and Robert Lehman, MD

Illustrated by Lia Cerizo

SASQUATCH BOOKS
SEATTLE

Contents

Introduction

Welcome to the book of questions asked by preteen boys (and girls—turn over and see the other side)! Who is asking these questions, you might ask? Julie Metzger and Rob Lehman have been leading classes for preteen boys and their dads, and preteen girls and their moms, on puberty and growing-up issues for more than twenty years. During these classes, we invite both the preteens and the adults to ask questions on cards so that we can answer them for the whole group, and we've saved every one of those questions. Some of the most frequently asked questions (*with a sprinkling of ones that made us smile*) asked by ten- to twelve-year-old boys appear on this side (those of ten- to twelve-year-old girls appear on the other).

Though these are all actual questions asked by preteens, we invite parents (yes, *especially* parents!) and educators and anyone else interested in what's on the minds of kids to read through these questions and our answers. Our responses are not meant to be exhaustive or the final word—just the opposite. Throughout the book we've tried to encourage kids to continue discussing these subjects in conversations with their parents and/or trusted adults in their lives. We believe that *families should be* the primary sexuality educators of children, and if these questions generate more questions, that's great.

Any differences you see between the boys' and the girls' sides reflect many years of answering preteens' questions and realizing that boys and girls may approach things differently. Hopefully we stay true to the tone that resonates with each gender.

Our most grateful thanks to all the preteen boys (and girls!) who were brave enough to submit a question and curious enough to sit through our classes and ask questions on subjects that were obviously important to them.

And thanks to our colleagues who reviewed the material to keep us **honest**, the kids who reviewed the material to keep us developmentally on-target, and our friends and families who made sure it stayed **interesting**.

And thanks *most of all* to Christopher for his unending support and to my parents, Roz and Ed Lehman, who patiently waited for me to pursue this project. Only parents could have enough love to wait so long and nudge so gently, yet persistently.

Dr Rob

RÓBERT LEHMAN, MD

Robert Lehman, MD, has devoted his professional career to adolescent health care. As a physician, his practice has focused on teenagers in many different clinical situations; he has worked for many years as an advocate for youth on the local and national levels; and as a member of the faculty at University of Washington, he has dedicated himself to teaching about adolescent health care needs to various health care professionals, parents, adolescents, and many other groups. For over twenty years, he and Julie Metzger have led classes for the public to promote parent-child communication in sexuality and other issues of adolescence through Great Conversations. For more information on classes, programs, and other resources, visit GreatConversations.com.

great **conversations**
about growing up. together.

1. Will **Puberty** Last My Whole Life?

. . . And Other Questions About Puberty

What exactly is puberty?
Can you feel puberty?

Puberty is the time when your body (and your *thoughts and emotions* too!) goes through all sorts of changes, mostly in your preteen and teenage years. *Can you feel it*? Not exactly, but you certainly can see that it's happening. Puberty is the time when your body changes from a boy's to a man's. It's set to start just like an alarm clock. At a certain age (determined by what you inherit from your birth mother and birth father), a message from your brain gives the signal. It tells a gland just under your brain, called the pituitary, to make a lot of a certain chemical, or hormone, that then travels all over your body. When it gets to your testicles, which are glands themselves, it tells them to make another hormone, called testosterone. This then *flows all through your body*, telling different parts to do different things—it tells your bones to grow faster, making you taller; it tells your muscles to get bigger and stronger; it tells your skin to grow hair in new places and produce oil; and it tells your voice box to grow longer, making your voice get lower. When you're all done, you will *look, act, and think, like a* man.

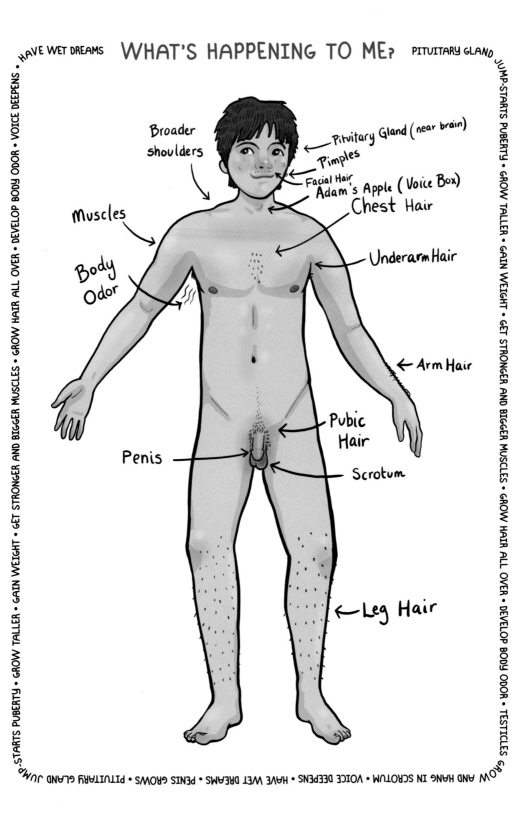

WHAT'S HAPPENING TO ME?

Broader shoulders

Pituitary Gland (near brain)

Pimples

Facial Hair

Adam's Apple (Voice Box)

Chest Hair

Muscles

Underarm Hair

Body Odor

Arm Hair

Pubic Hair

Penis

Scrotum

Leg Hair

How big is a HORMONE?

A hormone is a **chemical**. *You can't see it*, but it is carried by your blood to all parts of your body, including your brain, which also changes during puberty. Puberty starts when a lot of this hormone, called testosterone, gets released by the testicles and causes *all these amazing changes.*

. . . .

Is it WEIRD going through puberty?

Some guys wish they could stay just the way they were as kids, while other guys just can't wait to grow up. The thing is, everyone goes through puberty and has to experience the same changes. You might think that all this is weird because it's new, but you can be certain that *it's normal*—all the rest of the guys are doing it too.

. . . .

I wonder when I will have PUBERTY.
I wonder if it will be hard.

Most guys start puberty between the ages of ten and twelve, though a few can start earlier and a few later—and all of them are normal. The first thing you'll see is pubic hair, the hair growing around your penis. The next place you'll see hair is in your armpits, then on your arms, legs, and other places, with your full beard not coming in until much later. In the meantime, you'll be growing taller and getting bigger muscles and a lower voice. It might be confusing, surprising, or even astounding, but it's not hard—it's normal and *everybody goes through it!*

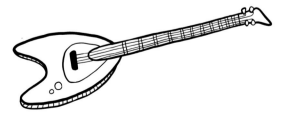

Can I still do things that I like to do (like building models)?

When your body—and the rest of you—grows up, you will naturally get interested in a lot of new things. Just because you add new interests doesn't mean you have to lose all the old ones.

A question I have is how much will I be like MY DAD?

We inherit most of what we are from our birth mothers and birth fathers—hair color, height, foot size, good looks, and lots of other things—but we are *a mix of both* of their families. So some of us take after one more than the other and some of us look like a little bit of both. But we are more than just what we inherit. We are influenced by our friends, by what we learn, and *by our experiences*—all of these things help make us unique individuals.

Why is puberty so EMBARRASSING?

Maybe puberty feels embarrassing because it has a lot to do with our bodies, and there are some parts of our bodies that we don't talk about very much, so it takes some getting used to. Maybe puberty feels embarrassing also because it's new and *because it happens no matter what*. Hopefully, after reading all these questions asked by other kids your age, it should be a little less embarrassing for you.

Is it OK to talk about this with my friends?

You bet. In fact, show them this book! You should also talk about this stuff with your **parents** or other trusted adults in your life—after all, they've definitely gone through this themselves and can help you **understand** it all to get through the changes that are coming. They want this to go well for you. The more you talk about **growing up** and the more questions you ask about it, the **less scary** it will seem. Here's a *fun exercise you can do*: ask a parent or other adult in your life to name three things that make them glad about growing up. The more adults you ask, the more things you'll learn to *look forward to* as you grow up yourself.

How do you know if you're NORMAL?

It's **normal** to worry about *whether you're normal!* Boys, men, girls, and women all think about this. Your friends might be a little ahead or a little behind you as they progress through puberty, but "normal" includes all of these paths to **growing up**. Some guys look at their friends or other guys at school and wonder why they seem to be so far ahead in **puberty**, or why they look so **different**. Throughout your preteen and teen years, you might see others who are taller or more muscular than you. Remember that the timing of puberty for you is set by what you *inherit from your birth parents*—not everyone starts at the same time or goes at the same speed. You could be the exact same age as another guy but be at a different place in puberty. That's okay—you'll all be adults in time. This is a terrific example of *different but normal*. And, if you're one of those boys who is progressing a little later than his friends, the good news is that you might continue **growing** even after they've stopped. So you might wind up taller than them in the long run!

Will puberty last my WHOLE LIFE?

Puberty is over when you no longer grow any taller. *For the average guy,* that's at about age eighteen, though some can stop sooner while others can continue **growing** after high school. But being a grown-up is a totally different thing, since it also involves the **responsibilities** of an adult. *And guess what?* Although puberty ends near the end of our teen years, our bodies (and minds!) continue to change throughout our lives. So you're not the only one growing and changing in the house—*everyone is*.

2. Do **Growth Spurts** Hurt?

. . . And Other Questions About Growing Taller

How tall will I grow?

How tall you grow depends on what you **inherited** from your birth mother and birth father. If you know your birth families on both sides, you can take a look at the adults and *get a good idea* of how tall you'll be. If one side of the family is **short** and the other is **tall**, you might be right in the middle, or closer to one or the other. Guys tend to *follow their dads* a little bit more closely than their moms. And if you don't know your birth parents on both sides, that's OK—you'll just have to be surprised, but you will probably wind up about average anyway. But another way to know is to ask your doctor or medical provider—they have something called a **growth chart**. It shows dots for each height as you are growing up, and they can predict fairly well how tall you'll be when you're fully grown.

Oh, and don't worry if your friends are growing faster than you—*you'll catch up*. The great news is that no matter what your final height is, you'll still be a **normal** grown-up guy.

Does diet pop and soda and coffee
STUNT YOUR GROWTH?

No. People have blamed lots of things for making them shorter than they wanted to be, but none of these by themselves can be blamed for that. Although some boys can have major health problems that may affect their height, most guys are as tall as their genetic inheritance from their parents will let them be. Getting good nutrition, *plenty of exercise*, and enough sleep will all help you to get as tall as your family genetics will allow.

Why are girls usually shorter than boys?

Height is just another one of the differences *between males and females*—in general, grown women are not as tall as grown men. That's not to say you don't occasionally see a very tall woman or a fairly short man—you do. And since girls usually start puberty a couple years before boys do and finish it faster (check it out on page 2 in the girls' section), you might find girls looking much taller or older than you when you're twelve or thirteen. But eventually guys will hit their *growth spurts* and catch up.

Do growth spurts hurt?

No! A growth spurt is that period of puberty when you appear to others to be *growing faster than a weed*. But it isn't that fast, and it doesn't hurt a bit. If you're an active guy, you might get growing pains (nighttime aches in your lower legs) early in puberty, but *they go away* as you continue to grow.

At what age do you stop growing?

The **average** guy stops growing around age **eighteen**, or during his senior year of high school. But that means half of all guys might stop sooner, while half continue to grow after high school. We stop **growing** because the same **hormone** that makes us grow faster in puberty (*testosterone*, remember?) also helps finish up that growing. Once you're done, *you're done*. You'll still make testosterone for all the other things you need it for, but it won't make you grow any more.

WOW! So this is what different but normal means.

3. How Come I Go to McDonald's a Lot but Don't Get Bigger?

. . . And Other Questions About Growing Bigger Muscles

When do guys start getting BIGGER MUSCLES?

Actually, your muscles have been growing, just like all the other parts of your body, *since you were born*. But when puberty starts and your body makes lots of testosterone, your muscles will grow faster and stronger than ever. It can start somewhat slowly; at the beginning of puberty, your body wants to get taller more than anything else. But when you get near the end of puberty and are not growing much taller anymore, you'll see your muscles change *a lot more*.

. . . .

Will I be STRONGER if I exercise?

Absolutely! Your muscles will need three things to get as big and strong as they can: a lot of good nutrition, those puberty hormones (like testosterone), and exercise. If you exercise, your muscles will get toned (that means they will be able to handle increased demands and be less likely to get strained). If you want to build them even bigger, then you'll need to do specific exercises for those muscles. Runners develop different muscles than gymnasts, and gymnasts will be different than baseball players. *Your heart is a muscle too*, and you can exercise it by doing most any activity that makes it beat faster. Different sports or exercises can have different effects on the strength, flexibility, coordination, and bulk of various muscles.

If you don't eat enough nutritional food but work out a lot, will you still GET BIG MUSCLES?

That would be like building a house with a lot of workers but not enough bricks or lumber! In order to **build** big muscles, you have to give them the **nutrients** they need. This certainly includes **protein**, but not *only* protein—it takes all the nutrients that you get from a *balanced diet.* Luckily, the testosterone that helps you build these muscles is also going to give you a larger appetite to make sure you take in what you need.

How come I go to McDonald's a lot but don't get BIGGER?

Just because you eat a lot of food doesn't mean you're eating the best **balance** of food. Try asking your parents to find out what *the best combination of foods* is for you that will help you **grow** to your max. You and your parents can also ask your doctor or medical provider for advice on what you need, and there are plenty of books and Internet sources for that information too. **Fast food** restaurants do have some good choices, but they can also have some unhealthy ones. And remember, if you eat too many **calories** but *don't exercise enough*, it might be your waist that grows more than your height or your muscles!

Is it bad to lift weights?

It depends. When you're just starting puberty, a lot of weight lifting won't do as much for your muscles, since your body is putting most of its efforts into *growing taller*. Also, this is a time when the growing parts of your bones (around your knees for your legs and at your shoulders and wrists for your arms) can potentially get injured. Lifting the *wrong way* or lifting *too much* weight too early could harm these growth centers. If you want to lift weights, don't just do it on your own—ask a coach or trainer for the proper and safe way to do it for the muscles you want to tone up.

Is it true that STEROIDS will really make your muscles bigger?

If you're talking about muscle-building steroids (and not some of the other kinds that people use to treat conditions like asthma), it's true. Combined with exercise, *they do build muscle*. But there are some major-league problems with using these types of steroids. I can think of five right off the top of my head: they are expensive, they hurt (since most need to be given by a shot), they are unfair in competition, they're illegal, and they can cause lots of bad side effects (like bad acne or a sick liver). So they may work, but they surely *don't seem worth it*.

4. Will You Burp **Deeper?**

. . . And Other Questions About Voice Change

I heard that your voice will change and go down, but that sometimes it will crack and go up. Why?

Along with all the other things that grow during puberty, your voice box (or *larynx*) gets longer too. The longer it gets, the lower the sound is when air moves through it. *It's just like with instruments*: tall bassoons have a lower sound than short clarinets, and long trombones sound much deeper than short trumpets. In fact, the voice box gets so big in guys that you can see its top end poking out on the front of your neck—some people call this the *Adam's apple*, though it doesn't look much like an apple to me. When you make testosterone, your voice box grows, and your voice sounds deeper. As for the voice cracking—anyone who is first learning how to play an instrument knows it takes time to get the sound right. Boys with voice boxes that are just starting to grow *have to get used to* that new sound going through— eventually the up-and-down cracking stops and people will be surprised at how low your voice sounds. Some guys will have very deep voices and could sing as basses, while other guys will have higher voices and could sing as tenors—and *there's everything in between*. Oh, and tall guys can have higher voices and shorter guys can have really deep ones. You'll only know what your voice will sound like *when you're done with puberty* and try it out.

How long does it take for your voice to change?

The **voice** starts to change not long after puberty begins, but it might be difficult to notice early on. Sometimes, in the course of a year, a guy can have a dramatic **change** in his voice but it's hard for him to notice *since he hears himself every day*. It's usually when Aunt Tillie visits and makes a comment about how grown-up you sound, or when you hear yourself on a recording, that you really take notice. Your voice is usually done changing *before you finish growing taller.*

Will you burp deeper?

Well, when I hear a baby burp, it sounds **softer** and higher pitched than when a **grown man** does it, so I guess you're right—but *that might come from* the man having a bigger stomach and longer distance for the burp to come out than from his longer voice box.

Why does your voice change when you get flabbier?

Things *other than puberty* can affect how your voice sounds. Some people find that gaining a lot of weight can make the voice sound **different**. Some notice that eating or drinking certain things, such as milk, can also affect it. Some people get **training** to make their voice sound better. One boy I knew tried to hurry up his voice change by standing in front of a mirror and practicing talking really deeply. It didn't work. I told him that his voice change would *definitely come all on its own,* just like the rest of puberty.

5. Does **Pubic** **Hair** Hurt When It Grows?

. . . And Other Questions About Body Hair

Where does the FIRST adolescent hair usually grow?

You'll usually first notice the hair that grows around your penis, which is commonly called your pubic area. Hair will eventually grow from your genitals (penis and scrotum) up to your belly button and *down to your thighs*. If you're really looking forward to all the body changes of puberty, that's the first place to look. Some guys can start to grow hair when they're as young as ten and some not until they're fourteen, but *they're all normal*. You might notice the hair starts out fairly straight and later gets somewhat curly. It also starts just at the base of the penis and later can show up on the legs and belly and even the butt, but those places can vary depending on how hairy you wind up being. After the pubic area, the second place hair usually grows is in your armpits, and after that, on the rest of your body.

Does pubic hair hurt when it grows?

Not at all. Some guys might be amazed at it, while some guys might think it looks weird. Still others will hardly notice. But everyone grows it as part of growing up. An occasional guy might wonder if people ever shave this hair off—yes, they can, but like other body hair, it will grow back and be a little itchy as it starts to regrow.

. . . .

Why do we have pubic hair anyway?

No one knows for sure. Think of how we evolved from species that were much hairier than we are, just like chimps and other primates are now. The species we evolved from were covered with hair *from top to bottom*, but we've lost that hair because we didn't need it—that's why we don't have hair on our elbows or knees. Why didn't the hair in our pubic area also go away? Some think it plays a role in making us more sexually attractive or in causing less friction down there, while some think it's to protect our genitals. *This might always be a mystery.*

. . . .

Does hair grow ON MY BUTT or is that a myth and is it a disease?

When guys go through puberty, hair can grow in *lots of places* it didn't before, such as your arms, legs, chest, back, the backs of your hands, the tops of your feet, and even on your butt. But some guys grow very little hair and some guys grow a lot. It's all normal, but the amount of hair you'll grow depends on how hairy your relatives are on both sides. Oh, and you'll grow hair in your nose and ears too. *Isn't that amazing?*

How come some kids get MORE HAIR than others?

You inherit the amount of hair you're going to have from your birth mother and birth father. If you know both sides of your family, you can look at them (the guys on both sides) to see about how hairy you're going to be. If they're really hairy on both sides, you're probably going to be too. If they're hardly hairy at all, then you probably won't be either. And if the guys on one side of your family are hairy and the guys on the other side aren't, you could be like one side or the other, or right in the middle. If you don't know both sides of your family (lots of guys don't for many reasons), *you can bet you're going to be pretty normal* with your hair. Oh, and the amount of hair a guy has has nothing to do with how manly he is. You will be a man no matter how much hair you have.

. . . .

Can you get TOO HAIRY on your arms and legs?

Unlike hair on your head and hair on your face, which will get longer and longer if you don't cut it, hair on other parts of your body just tends to stop at a certain length, depending on where it is. So, you really don't have to worry that you'll have to comb your arms and legs too!

. . . .

Why on earth do we have hair in our ears?

Great question! A lot of guys wonder about this. Some people think that we have hair in our ears to prevent dirt from getting in there and clogging them up—just like nose hair helps to prevent dust from getting into our noses and possibly our lungs. But most guys think that ear hair is just annoying. Both men and women get nose hair, but only guys get ear hair. *Lucky us!*

Why do you get facial hair?
When does it grow?

The same **hormone** that makes us grow taller, get bigger muscles, and have lower voices (*testosterone*) also makes hair grow during puberty in certain places it never grew before. Your **face** is just one of those places. Your **facial hair** starts to grow when puberty begins but it doesn't come in fully until much later—for some guys, not until their twenties! Some guys will grow hair early, while some will grow it later; some guys will wind up having a lot, while others won't have as much; some will have dark hair, while some will have very light hair. A lot of these differences depend on what you **inherit** from your birth parents, so you'll probably end up looking *a lot like the men in your family*.

· ·

Does **SHAVING** affect hair growth
anywhere (not just your face)?

Although lots of guys might think that shaving speeds up hair growth, that's a **myth**. Shaving hair makes no difference in how fast it's going to grow back—whether that's on your head, your face, or anywhere else. *Hair is on its own schedule.*

Will your beard grow your hair color?

Usually. Sometimes it can be a little **lighter** or **darker**, and when you get old, it can turn gray earlier or later than the rest of your hair. The color has a lot to do with your family and what color hair you inherited from your birth mom and birth dad. Oh, and the hair on your beard *might feel a little different* from the hair on your head.

. . . .

How do you grow a GOATEE?

Easy! You **shave** away everything that isn't a goatee! *The good thing is*, if you don't like what you see, you can always let it **grow out** or shave it off.

. . . .

When will I have to begin shaving?

Many guys will see *some soft hair growing* above their **upper lips** early in puberty. You can start shaving as soon as you have hair to shave. One of the cool things about facial hair is that you can **decide** what you want to look like . . . and change your mind. Do you want a clean-shaven face, or do you want a long

beard? Or maybe a moustache you can twist around your ears?! You can try something out, like a soul patch, then shave it off if you don't want it anymore.

· ·

Can I completely GET RID OF facial hair?

Though it might be annoying to have to shave all the time if you don't want a beard or moustache, there's really no way to make facial hair go away forever. Think of it as *just part of being a guy.*

· ·

If you have a light beard, will shaving it off and starting again make it come in thicker?

That's a myth! Shaving early or shaving a lot will not make your beard grow faster, or thicker, or better. *Don't bother shaving* if there's nothing there to shave yet! It will grow in eventually, so *be patient.* Some guys inherit really thick beards from their families, while other guys have very light beards that don't need to be shaved as often. Just be patient—many guys don't start getting their full adult beards until their twenties.

· ·

How do you do it (I mean SHAVING)?

You can choose a razor blade (check out all the types there are in a drugstore) or an electric shaver. You can shave dry, but using something to lubricate your skin first (like water, soap, or shaving cream) can help keep you from cutting yourself. Then you can choose where to start and which way to move the razor, though *you'll learn which way cuts better* as you go along. A great way to learn is to watch your dad or uncle or grandfather or any grown-up guy you feel close to. See what he does and ask him why he shaves that way.

What is the point of aftershave?

I've wondered about that myself! In the old days, when razors weren't as well made and guys routinely *cut themselves* while shaving, products like aftershave were splashed on to prevent infections and perhaps to help cuts heal faster. These days, both razor blades and electric shavers rarely nick your skin, so I suppose it's more to make you smell nice.

. . . .

Is there a way to STOP the hair on my body?

Some people don't like the hair that grows with puberty because they like their bodies the way they are, but this is *just part of growing up*, along with getting taller and stronger and all the rest. Eventually we get used to our new adult bodies. Some people try to remove hair by shaving it or using creams that shed hair, but most of these are temporary, and the hair grows back.

. . . .

Why do men GO BALD?

Some guys inherit the tendency to lose the hair on their heads from their families. Scientists are still trying to figure this out—it has something to do with one's hormones and how they act on one's hair—and they haven't figured out how to completely stop it yet. Luckily, guys can look great even with little or no hair. But if you're still concerned about it, maybe they'll discover a way *to stop balding* by the time you get to that age.

6. How **Smelly** Will I Get?

. . . And Other Questions About Body Odor

How does BODY ODOR start?

Body odor is another one of those things we all face when we grow up. When the **testosterone** starts pumping through your body to make you taller and stronger, it also changes your skin. Not only does your skin grow hair in certain places, it also produces more **oil** and **sweat**. Oil keeps our skin from getting too dry and sweat *keeps us from getting too hot*. But sometimes we make too much oil and too much sweat. When that happens, the **bacteria** on our skin (which have always lived there but haven't caused trouble) start to multiply as they feast on all that oil and sweat. It's the bacteria that make that very interesting odor.

Armpits smell particularly bad because they have many **sweat glands** and **oil glands**, and are nice dark places where **bacteria** like to grow. There are other similar places on your body—*like your feet and your groin*—where bacteria like to grow too. But many guys just seem to smell bad all over.

How SMELLY will I get?

Your odor is very **individual**, and it's affected by how active you are and what you do about it. But let's just say that teenage guys

can get pretty smelly. Some guys wonder why they can't tell how smelly they are. Our noses become accustomed to a bad smell if it's there all the time. So, you might have to *rely on someone else to let you know* when you start smelling bad. Don't ask your friend to put his nose in your armpit! Don't ask your dog—he loves you no matter how bad you stink. And definitely don't ask your first date—not if you ever expect a second date! Ask someone close to home who cares about you and is good at picking up odors, like a parent or another adult with whom you live.

Unlike acne, which tends to get better when you grow up, *body odor is something all active guys* have to deal with their whole life. The more active you are, the more you'll need to watch for body odor. Most adult guys take showers daily and use some form of deodorant, but you can make that decision for yourself when you reach adulthood.

. . . .

How do you tell a friend they need deodorant?

You can tell him what you learned to help with your own body odor. First, the best thing is to wash off as much of the sweat, oil, and bacteria as you can. That means a *shower or bath* with soap. But some guys need something more, such as deodorant or antiperspirant. These are products that you buy in a grocery store or drugstore that you rub in your armpits to cover up the smell. They come in many different scents and styles. Antiperspirants not only cover up your smell, but also have a chemical in them called aluminum that stops you from sweating for a while. It's best for guys just starting puberty to stick with just washing when they have some smell. Guys further along in puberty might want to use deodorants or, later in teenage years, antiperspirants. If you're curious, *ask your parents* what they use and why they chose it. I'm sure your strong-smelling friend will get the message after hearing your advice.

7. What is the Point of Getting **Zits?**

. . . And Other Questions About Pimples

What is the point of getting zits?

No one gets zits because they want to, and zits serve **no useful purpose** to my knowledge! But I can tell you *how we get them.* That same hormone, **testosterone**, that guys make so much of in puberty, causes a lot of changes in their bodies. One of these changes is that your skin makes more **oil**—more oil than you need to keep your skin healthy. Your skin makes so much oil that you can see it on your forehead and other places as the day goes on. This oil tends to fill in tiny holes in your skin, called **pores**, which blocks them, resulting in bumps we call **pimples**, *acne*, or *zits*.

. . . .

Does everyone FOR SURELY get acne?

I've never met a **grown-up** who didn't have at least some **pimples** at some time in his life. Some guys will have only a few while other guys can get **a lot**. Although the tendency to have acne generally runs in families, other things probably determine if you'll get a lot of **acne** or just a little—so looking at your brother or sister or asking your birth parents if they had bad acne probably won't predict exactly how yours will be. *The important thing* is that nothing can keep you from ever having a zit, no matter what they say in a television commercial. What you need to do is take care of your skin when you have zits so that your *face looks as good as before* when they eventually go away.

. . . .

What are BLACK AND WHITE HEADS?

Once your pores get *blocked with oil*, the stuff inside the zit can build up (making it look white or black) or get infected (making it look red and feel tender). Sometimes an infected zit will need a special medicine, but mostly these pimples just need to be cared for (see page 27).

. . . .

Is acne only on your face?

That's the place people care about most, since it's the place that's *most obvious to others*. But you can get acne on your shoulders, back, chest, and even on your thighs. In fact, you can get zits anywhere, but these are the usual trouble spots.

. . . .

Do any foods make acne WORSE?

Although *lots of people might think so*, it's not true that there are foods that can make acne worse. People might get that idea because certain foods (like nuts and candy) have a lot of oils in them, and it's oil on your skin that causes acne. But the oils in food and the oil on your skin are different. The truth is that your skin makes the acne-causing oil no matter how much or little oil you are eating in your food.

What happens when you have a zit at school and a girl is grossed out?

Some people are embarrassed by their zits and think everyone is staring at them. They'll try things like combing their hair over their foreheads (that could make it worse!) or covering their faces with some cream to hide the zits (if the cream contains oil, that could also make it worse!). Remember, *everyone gets zits* at some point or another. So, the best thing to do is to take care of your zits and try to keep from getting too many of them (see page 27). And, by the way, *girls get zits too* (see pages 12–14 on the girls' side).

· ·

Did you play any sports in high school or college that made you get acne?

You're probably asking that because you heard that sports can make acne worse. Well, it's not the sports, actually, but the helmets you wear while you play sports that *can cause your skin to make even more oil*. The key is washing your face after practice to make sure that wearing a helmet doesn't make things worse.

· ·

If you don't wash your face will zits STAY FOREVER?

No, zits will eventually go away. The main reason to take care of your skin is to prevent zits from getting infected, because when a zit gets infected, it can lead to scarring. Scars are those marks or pits you see on some grown-ups even though they no longer have any zits. You can make your zits better, but you can't get rid of those scars.

At what age do zits go away?

Sorry to tell you, but *grown-ups can get zits too*. But the good news is that they'll be much less of a problem when you finish puberty, so take the time during puberty to really **take care of your skin** so that it looks good later.

. . . .

Does TOOTHPASTE remove zits?

No, it doesn't (but it does a good job on your teeth!). You might hear of a lot of things kids have tried to make their acne better, but most of them don't work. The first thing you need to do is get rid of as much of that **oil** as possible. **Washing your face** once or twice a day with water and soap (any soap—it doesn't have to be fancy) either at the sink or in the shower or bath will be absolutely the best thing you can do to reduce the number of pimples on your face. If you're doing that, but you are still getting pimples, then go to the store or pharmacy with your parent and pick up an **acne medicine**. Check out the ingredients for something called *benzoyl peroxide 5%*, or just BP 5%, which is the most important thing to help your pimples. Something called *salicylic acid* can also be useful. If the medicine has alcohol or a ton of other chemicals but neither of these chemicals, then it might not help your face no matter how much it costs. And, if you're washing daily and using one of these products and you're still getting a lot of pimples, then you can ask a doctor or nurse practitioner to prescribe a **more powerful** medicine to help you. But most kids don't need anything like this if they simply wash their faces and use the products mentioned above.

8. Does Food Affect Your Penis Size?

. . . And Other Questions About Your Penis and Erections

How and why do penises grow?

From the time you're born, *your body is growing*. When you enter puberty, every-thing grows even **faster**. That includes your penis as well as almost all of the other parts of you. You might notice your penis getting a little **longer** at first, then even-tually a little **wider**—but most boys don't notice much change until one day they take a look and wonder, "**Wow!** When did that happen?" You might also notice other changes in this area, including hair growing around your penis, your testicles getting bigger, and your scrotum (the sac holding the testicles) getting darker. All of this is totally normal, and I'll explain it all further on.

When does a penis STOP GROWING/ reach its top size?

Usually when you **stop growing taller**, which is the end of puberty, your **penis** stops growing too. For most boys, that's at the end of high school, but the exact timing can vary. Some things (like your beard, see page 18) can still continue to change even after you stop growing.

Does PENIS SIZE matter?

A *lot* of guys spend *too much* time worrying about whether their penis is **big enough**. Actually, your penis will be absolutely the **right size** to do the things it's supposed to do—*urinate* and *have sex* (more on that later!). Some guys might think that having a bigger penis makes you manlier, but *that's not true at all*. Other guys might think that you'll be more popular if you have an enormous penis, but popularity has nothing to do with penis size. Besides, what would you do with a four-foot penis anyway?! You might hear people say they have some surefire way to make your penis bigger faster. *Don't believe them!* Your penis will grow in its own time. Don't worry—yours will be normal and *do what it needs to do*.

....

Does food affect your penis size?

Nope. Nor does pulling on it, making wishes, or changing the type of underwear you wear! It will get *as big as it will get*, and it will work just fine.

....

Why does my penis look DIFFERENT from some other guys?

Well, it could have to do with **circumcision**. Check out the picture (page 37) so that this makes sense. Every guy in the world is born with a thin piece of skin that covers the tip of his penis (called a **foreskin**). Some parents choose to have this piece of skin removed soon after birth by a doctor or a religious person. If this happens, we call it a circumcised penis. If not, it's an uncircumcised penis. Some parents choose circumcision because it's a **religious** custom, some do it because they *think it's healthier*, and some choose to circumcise because the dad was circumcised and the parents want the son to look the same.

If a boy isn't circumcised, will it affect his life?

Like we talked about previously, *penises are designed to do two things*: to **pee** and to **have sex**. Whether you are circumcised or not, your penis will be able to do both of these things just fine. Millions of guys still have their foreskins and millions don't. The only thing is, if you still have a foreskin, it's good to **clean** underneath when taking a shower or bath (just like cleaning any other part of your body). Slide the foreskin back as much as it will go comfortably, clean underneath, then let it go back where it was. *Easy!*

Is it painful to have a circumcision when you're 16 years old?

It **hurts** any time part of your body gets cut. *When it's done on babies*, sometimes the doctor will **numb** the area first, but babies are very forgiving and forget very quickly, since the cut heals up fast. In some cases (again because of tradition or because of an unusual medical problem with the foreskin) boys may get a circumcision when they're older. Usually, these guys are **asleep** for this surgery or numbed really well.

When I rub my penis, I get a STRANGE FEELING. Why?

You also might notice that your penis **changes shape** when you do this. Let me explain. You might think that **erections** have only to do with sex, but guys get erections *even before they're born!* You have special nerve endings around your penis that, when touched in a certain way, signal special openings in your penis to fill with blood, causing it to get bigger, **harder**, and point upward. When you stop touching the penis, the extra blood leaves, and your penis goes back to the shape it was before. Baby boys get erections when their diapers go on and off, and young boys get them occasionally when washing their penises. But when a guy gets to puberty, the whole thing gets super sensitive—almost anything can make the penis erect. Erections can happen at any time—when you're in class, when you're reading, or when you're simply staring at the wall. *This is normal.*

And then, there's *another* way guys in puberty get erections—by thinking sexual thoughts. This usually only happens when you've gone through puberty and then start to have thoughts you've never had before. These thoughts are *totally* normal, and all guys have them. Sexual thoughts can cause erections even when you don't touch your penis. To most guys, touching their penises feels pretty good. After puberty, this touching can eventually result in ejaculation, or when the semen loaded with sperm comes out the end of your penis (see page 38). When this happens to a guy while he's sleeping, we call it a wet dream (see page 39), which is a natural thing that happens occasionally during puberty to almost all guys. When the guy is awake, we call it masturbation (see page 41).

. . . .

How do you control HARD-ONS?

Sometimes erections can happen at awkward times (like when you're asked to stand in front of the class or when you're walking down the hallway). There's not much to do except *wait for it to go down*, though some guys will turn away for a minute or try to think of something else (not sexual things). When you get older, you'll automatically learn to have more control over them. By the way, guys have lots of words—slang words like "hard-on"—for erections. You'll hear other guys use these words, and you might use them yourself. That's okay, as long as you know the real word, too.

A question I have is, can you have an erection if you have to pee?

Guys sometimes get concerned about things getting **mixed up** down there. The good news is that your body is designed so that doesn't happen. When a guy has an erection, *he can't pee*. And when he's urinating, there will be **no surprise** erections. Clever, huh?

. . . .

Every time you get an erection, does semen come out?

No, guys have plenty of erections that come and go without anything more happening. But keep reading further about **semen** and when it comes out.

. . . .

Is it hard to be social when having an erect penis?

I suppose it could be. The thing is, depending on the type of pants you're wearing, most other people **can't tell**, even if *you* know you're having one. Then again, it could be *really difficult* to dance with one, or to have a serious conversation with your grandparents while having one!

9. If You Never Have Sex, Will **Your Balls** Just Keep Getting Bigger and Bigger?

. . . And Other Questions About Testicles, Sperm, and Related Things

What's in the testicle?

A **testicle** (also known as a *testis* or a *ball*) is a gland that makes testosterone, the hormone that makes us taller, stronger, hairier, and smellier. It also makes sperm. Sperm are single cells that, when combined with an egg from a woman, make a new person. When your testicles get the hormone message from the pituitary (that gland near your brain) telling them that puberty is starting, they start pumping out lots of **testosterone**, and at the same time, they make lots of sperm. Each day, a guy's testicles can make millions of sperm. Sperm get stored for a couple of days and then if you don't use them, your body destroys them and makes brand new ones.

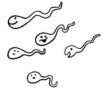

Are sperm actually ALIVE and do they know where to go?

Sperm are definitely alive, and they are some of the few cells in our bodies that can move around on their own. Sperm have tails and look like tadpoles. They also swim like tadpoles by shaking their tails back and forth. But they *don't have eyes and they don't have brains*, so they don't know where to swim—they just swim. If sperm are going to be used—like in wet dreams (see page 39), masturbation (see page 41), or sexual intercourse (see page 70)—they swim up two tubes, each called a *vas*, which bring them up from the testicles to the urethra so they can come out the end of the penis.

Does one testicle make one type of sperm and the other makes the other?

Most of us do have two testicles, and you're right—there are two types of sperm. Half of your sperm will have an X chromosome and would produce a *baby girl*; the other half have a Y chromosome in order to make a *baby boy*. Both testicles make both kinds. For more on that, see the chapter on pregnancy starting on page 84.

If you never have sex, will your balls just keep getting bigger and bigger?

No! A guy would look pretty silly having testicles *the size of beach balls!* Testicles are little factories—their job is to make testosterone and sperm. To do their job, they do start growing when you start puberty, but when they get to adult size at the end of puberty, that's it.

If you get hit in the testes, will you get damaged?

Most guys at some point get **accidentally** hit or kicked in their testicles—and they learn really quickly not to let that happen ever again! Guys have a lot of special **nerve** endings around their testicles reminding them to *protect them* and not let them get hit. If a guy does get hit, usually it just **hurts** a lot but gets better on its own. If it's a major hit, though, the testicle could be damaged. If a guy loses one testicle—by getting hit like that or having a disease like cancer just like Lance Armstrong—or if he was only born with one, that's okay. One **testicle** can do the job of two if it has to.

What does it mean when balls (or testes) drop?

This may be a real **surprise**, but our testicles start out deep inside our bellies, not in the **scrotum**, or **sac**. Just a few weeks before we're born, our testicles move down through our groins and pop into our scrotums, where they should be when we're born. (Occasionally a testicle will get stuck along the way, and it needs to be helped along with surgery, or removed if it gets stuck deep inside.) The reason we have our testicles outside our bodies instead of deep inside where they could be protected is that they need to be a little **cooler** than our bodies in order to make sperm. As a guy moves through puberty, his testicles grow to their full size and **hang** at the bottom of the scrotum, therefore appearing to "drop." Once your testicles get into your scrotum, they can still move around a little. If they're too cold (like if you're standing in the ocean in the winter), the testicles will rise up as high as they can in the scrotum in order to get **warmer**. On the other hand, if they're too hot (like if you're really hot in the middle of summer), the testicles can hang really low in the scrotum to try to get as cool as possible.

What if one testicle grows bigger than the other?

Occasionally, one testicle can be slightly bigger than the other, and in almost all guys, the left testicle hangs lower than the right one. But, rarely, a guy can get a problem on his testicles or in his scrotum, so we tell all guys to *gently feel their testicles* every so often to make sure they're all right. There are several reasons a guy could feel something not right there—and the scariest thing would be cancer—but this is extremely rare and could be fully cured if found early enough. That's where you come in—you should check regularly to make sure your testicles are okay. *At your next physical exam*, you can ask your healthcare provider to talk about that with you.

. . . .

I have a lump in my nipple. Does that mean I have breast cancer?

Aha, you've discovered one of the secrets about boys' puberty! First of all, don't worry—this isn't cancer. And you're not turning into a girl (though some guys needlessly do worry about that)! Remember all that testosterone that you start making in puberty that makes you taller, stronger, smellier, and hairier? Well, as it turns out, all guys in the world make both male hormones (like testosterone) and female hormones. What makes us *guys* is that we make a whole lot more male hormone than female. But when we're in puberty, our body is pumping out more of all of these hormones, so we might produce a little more of the teensy amount of female hormones than ordinarily. About half of all guys see a little enlargement of one breast or both. Usually, it just feels like a lump under the nipple, but sometimes it could be a little larger. The good news is that *this goes away all by itself* in almost all guys when puberty is over.

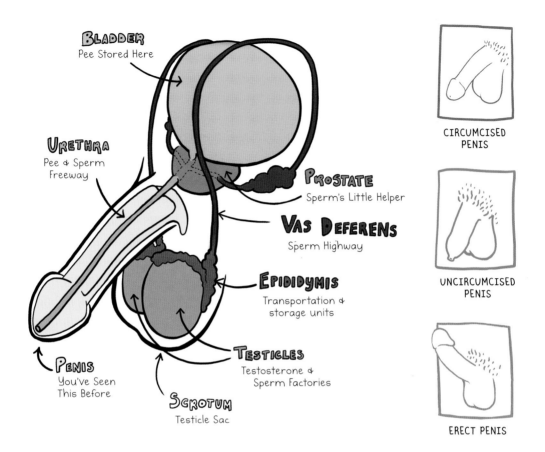

BLADDER
Pee Stored Here

URETHRA
Pee & Sperm
Freeway

PROSTATE
Sperm's Little Helper

VAS DEFERENS
Sperm Highway

EPIDIDYMIS
Transportation &
storage units

PENIS
You've Seen
This Before

TESTICLES
Testosterone &
Sperm Factories

SCROTUM
Testicle Sac

CIRCUMCISED
PENIS

UNCIRCUMCISED
PENIS

ERECT PENIS

What does the semen do? I only got info on the sperm.

The sperm is really, **really tiny**—you can't even see one without a microscope. It's also a great swimmer and goes fast considering its small size. But it has no reserve of energy, so it would run out of energy if it didn't get an energy boost from something along the way. Sperm gets its energy boost from **semen**. Semen is a special liquid made by a gland called a **prostate** (and nearby structures called seminal vesicles). It keeps the sperm moist and provides sugars and other nutrients to give them the **energy** to *stay alive and finish their trip*. You can't see sperm, but you can see semen; it's white, and it looks like mucus.

Why do I hear my grandfather complain about the prostrate?

I think he's probably complaining about the prostate! That's an important gland for making the semen that nourishes the sperm. As a guy gets older, his prostate can have a harder time doing its job, so it might get larger to produce the same amount of semen. This could wind up pressing on his urethra, the tube that takes urine from the bladder to the penis, making it *harder for him to pee* (see the picture on page 37 so this makes sense). This is why young guys can often pee farther and stronger than their dads and grandfathers.

. . . .

How does the sperm come out of the penis? Does it pee out or does it automatically come out?

When sperm are going to be used (during wet dreams, masturbation, or sex—see Chapter 10 and Chapter 14 for more on those), your internal muscles help them get up to the prostate to get surrounded by the semen, then continue to help them along to the end of your penis, using the same route urine would take (but semen is different than urine!). Urine and semen with sperm never mix—only one can take that route at a time. When sperm and semen do come out (when your penis is erect), we call that ejaculation. It happens in a few spurts—maybe *a teaspoon total*—then it's over, and the penis goes back to its normal shape.

. . . .

What are JOCK STRAPS for?

When guys play certain sports, they wear jock straps under their shorts in order to protect their testicles. Jock straps not only keep the testicles closely tucked in so they won't get easily hit, but they also make it more comfortable to run. *Jiggling testicles can be a real annoyance!*

10. I Don't Remember **Dreaming**. Am I Still Going to Enter Puberty?

. . . And Other Questions About Wet Dreams and Masturbation

What is a WET DREAM?
Is it really due to a dream?

After puberty begins, a guy's reproductive system does something I like to call "testing things out." Now that the guy is making testosterone and sperm, the system tries it out, at night, when the guy's asleep—in fact, when he's dreaming. Guys get erections when they dream (no matter what they're dreaming about). During a wet dream, the sperm come up from the testicles, join together with the semen, and come out the end of the penis together. Some guys might sleep through the whole thing and find a dried spot on their pajamas or sheets or underwear. It might look like he's peed in bed, but it's nothing like that. Other guys might wake up right after it happens and discover it: "Wow! What's that? Oh, yeah, *it's that wet dream thing.*" It's totally normal and part of a guy growing up.

I don't remember dreaming. Am I still going to enter puberty?

You bet. A lot of people **can't remember** their dreams. That's okay—you're still dreaming even if you don't remember it, and that's when a **wet dream** happens. And not every guy remembers having a wet dream—that's okay too. *You'll still enter puberty at the normal time.*

Am I going to do this every night for the rest of my life?

Absolutely not. Some guys experience only a couple of wet dreams, while others have a bunch during puberty. Adult guys can occasionally get one, but not often. Somehow, once you get older, your body doesn't need to do this anymore.

. . . .

A boy at school says wet dreams are bad and he'd never had one.

Wet dreams are not bad—they're normal. Almost all grown-up guys can remember having them. *It is just part of being a guy*. Does every guy have them? Well, some guys can't remember having one, but maybe they slept right through it and never noticed. That's okay too.

. . . .

What does it mean to 'JACK OFF'?

"Jack off" is a slang term for masturbation that you might hear. Guys use a lot of slang words for anything to do with sexuality. Why? Maybe because people *don't often talk about these things* or because some people say you shouldn't talk about them. When people are told not to talk about things, they often come up with other terms to say the same thing. Some of these are funny, but some, especially when boys use slang words for parts of the girl's body, can be disrespectful and hurtful. Is it okay to use slang words occasionally? That depends on who you're talking to, but remember that some people might not find them funny. Oh, and *be sure you know the real word* for things before you use the slang word.

Now back to masturbation. This is when a guy touches or rubs his penis until it becomes erect and then keeps rubbing it until he ejaculates (when the sperm come out in the semen). It's not something that happens by itself—it's something he chooses to do. Guys do this mostly because it **feels good**, though other guys say it's a way of *working out their sexual feelings*. After a guy ejaculates, his penis returns to its relaxed state.

. . . .

Is there such a thing as TOO MUCH masturbation?

First of all, masturbation is a **choice** guys make. Can a guy choose *not* to do it? Sure. But the overwhelming majority of guys do choose to masturbate at some point in their lives. Why? Because it **feels good.** You might wonder why, if it feels so good, guys don't masturbate a thousand times a day. Well, first, because they can't. It takes **body energy** to ejaculate and you just can't do it that often. The body needs time to *recharge energy* and *sperm*. More importantly, there are many other things you need to get done during the day—eating, sleeping, going to school, playing, and spending time with family and friends. Another very important issue is that in some families, some communities, and some faiths, masturbation is not felt to be an acceptable thing to do. Your parents and the other adults in your lives may have some definite feelings and thoughts about this—so, *as awkward as it might be*, you might consider having a conversation about this with them.

. . . .

If you masturbate before puberty, will your dong be smaller?

If a guy rubs his penis before puberty, he might get an erection but probably won't ejaculate since sperm isn't being made yet. But certainly, it **won't** make your penis **smaller**, or do *anything else bad to you*. In order to persuade boys not to touch their penises, some adults make up things that could happen to you if you masturbate. *No*, masturbating won't make you crazy. *No*, masturbating won't make you go blind. *No*, masturbating won't give you more pimples or make you grow hair on your palms. And it definitely *won't* make your penis fall off! **Nothing bad** happens to your body if you masturbate, and you can't tell by looking at someone if they've ever done it.

11. Do Girls Fart?

. . . And Other Questions That Boys Have About Girls and Their Bodies

Do girls get the same information about all this stuff as we do?

Hopefully! Of course, girls might have **different** questions than boys do, and be interested in slightly different things than boys are. You can read through the girls' section of this book to see what's different and what's the same.

Do girls going through puberty realize that boys are changing also?

I'm sure they do. Of course, it's okay to tell them what you're feeling during all these changes—just so they know your view of things. But when people are changing so fast in puberty and just learning how to manage their new **bodies**, they tend to focus on **themselves** a lot. We all need to pay some attention to *what's happening to others around us* too.

How come girls' hair is longer?

Because they **wear it** that way! It depends on the **culture** you're in and what's popular at the time, but in our culture, girls tend to wear their hair longer than guys do. However, *in some other cultures*, guys also grow their hair really long. And in still others, girls cut it short.

. . . .

How come some girls have hair like a moustache?

All girls have some male-type **hormones** in their bodies—they make these hormones in various glands around their body. These are the hormones that help them grow taller, grow hair, and also contribute to body odor and pimples. Some women do grow just **a little hair** above their lips as a result (but *will never grow a beard* like you). It doesn't affect their functioning as a female, but many don't like the look, so they'll do various things to remove the hair. It's about the same thing, only in reverse, as guys having a little breast enlargement during puberty (see page 36).

. . . .

Can girls hold their pee?

Of course. Girls have **bladders** *just like guys do*. The bladder is a hollow muscle shaped like a ball. It fills with urine as the kidneys make it, stretching to hold as much as it can. When it gets full, you empty your bladder by letting the urine flow out the urethra (that hole at the end of your penis). Girls have a urethra too, only much shorter than yours since they don't have a penis. Because women are generally somewhat **smaller** than men, they might have slightly smaller bladders and therefore can't hold as much pee.

How do girls pee? Do girls pee out of their butt?

You might have noticed that guys can either sit down or stand up to pee, but girls have to sit down. Though guys can point their penis in the right direction when they pee (hopefully!), girls don't have penises, so their pee can really only go straight down. That's why they always need to sit when peeing. Guys have two openings in the pubic/butt area: the urethra at the end of their penis for both urine and semen (at different times, of course) and the *anus* for moving their bowels. Girls have three: the *urethra* for urinating, the vagina for sexual intercourse, and the *anus* for moving their bowels (see the picture on page 31 on the girls' side).

Why do girls go to the bathroom in groups?

It might be how we're built differently or how we learn to do things differently. Girls enjoy being with others and sharing their *feelings and thoughts*. Boys, especially when it comes to bathroom visits, *tend to do their own thing* and not do a lot of communicating. Can you think of other ways we act differently, or can you observe people to see if you notice some of these differences? It makes people laugh sometimes to see just how different the other gender can be.

Are girls circumcised?

Generally, girls are not circumcised. In certain cultures in Africa, there is a custom called "female circumcision," but in this country it's very rare. When we talk about circumcision here, people think of the removal of the foreskin on guys (see page 29).

Do GIRLS FART?

Yes, they do, just as much as guys. It's possible you might not have noticed since girls might try harder than boys *not to do it in front of other people*. Girls burp too, by the way, and have stomach noises, just like us. There are more things that are the same about girls' and boys' bodies than are different, as it turns out.

. . . .

What do BREASTS have to do with all this?

A lot of people wonder about this. Girls' breasts develop and change during puberty, and their function is to eventually provide milk to feed babies. For many females, having breasts is an important part of being a woman (see Chapter 5 on the girls' side to read what they say about them). For many men, breasts are an important part of what makes them *sexually attracted to women*, though they're certainly not the only part that attracts them. The key is getting to know all the other things that make you attracted to someone—not just one part of their body.

. . . .

Why do girls have boobs but boys don't?

Biologically, girls have breasts in order to feed babies. Guys don't give birth to babies, nor do they have much estrogen to make breasts like women do. We do have nipples, however, which are left over from evolution. Sometimes guys' breasts can temporarily get bigger during puberty (see page 36). Oh, and as for using slang words for parts of the body—*be careful*. Though you might hear other guys referring to breasts with slang words, a lot of women may find it disrespectful.

Do girls have anything similar to erections?

Well, *sort of*. In front of their urethral openings (where they pee from), women have a little structure called a **clitoris**. Although only about the size of a pea, the clitoris can get slightly bigger when a woman gets sexually **excited**—just like a guy's penis. And like a penis, the clitoris is **sensitive** to touch. What this means is that, just like your penis, if touched gently, *it can feel good*, but if touched roughly, it can be really uncomfortable!

. . . .

When girls masturbate, what comes out? How do girls masturbate?

Girls can do something similar, although they don't have a penis to rub. Instead, they have a **clitoris**, a small structure near the outside of the vagina. When rubbed, this can give them a **good feeling** too. But *they don't ejaculate* since they don't make sperm or semen, and masturbating has no effect on their eggs. Girls don't report masturbating as much as boys do, but they can do it too. (See what girls say about masturbating on page 70 on the girls' side.)

. . . .

How do you know when a woman is having a period?

Mostly, *you'll just have to ask her!* To learn exactly what a period is and how women take care of them, check out Chapter 7 on the girls' side (since they have *plenty* of questions about that themselves).

Does it hurt to put a tampon in or the boy equivalent?

A tampon is something girls might use to control their periods. By the "boy equivalent," I imagine you mean a penis during sexual intercourse. (You can *check over on the other side* to see how putting in a tampon is explained to girls on page 33.)

. . . .

Do boys have periods like girls?

No. To have a period, you have to have a **uterus**, the purpose of which it is to have a **baby**. Since guys don't have a uterus, they *can't have a period* (see Chapter 7 on the girls' side for more on this).

. . . .

Why do girls always think they're FAT when they're not?

A lot of girls are raised to feel it's important to **look good** to others. Sometimes they might **worry** about this too much. If a girl or woman thinks that it's necessary to be thin for someone to like her, then she might worry about it a lot. It's also true that our **media** (like television commercials and magazine ads) tends to show women *a lot thinner than they really are*. Some women take that as an example of how they should look and try hard to get there, even though that's not the way their bodies are built and it could be unhealthy for them to be that thin. This is something you *as a guy might help them with*—by **complimenting** them on the way they look and making sure they know there are lots of other things about them that are also important to you besides their appearance.

How do girls get to be so SEXY?

Sexy is in the *eye of the beholder!* What is sexy for one person might not be at all for another. Maybe another person becomes **attractive** to you when they start to look grown-up or make themselves look nice. Or maybe you are finding another person attractive because you are **changing** yourself. (Remember that testosterone is changing our brains too, and causes us to have new thoughts—thoughts of attraction. See page 52.) Actually, it's probably a *combination of both.*

. . . .

Why do girls always want to be so CLEAN?

Girls differ from guys in many ways, but remember that not all girls are the same, just like not all guys are the same. Besides their **genetic** and body **differences**, boys and girls are also frequently raised differently. Depending on the culture and the family, boys are encouraged to do certain things and act certain ways, while girls might be *encouraged differently.* Keeping things in order and clean could be one of those things. Again, there are certainly girls who are **messy** and certainly boys who are quite **neat**. Oh, and while you think of them as too clean, they might be thinking of you as too dirty or disorderly! It's all a matter of the way you look at people.

. . . .

Why are girls so chatty and STRANGE?

Girls tend to be more **vocal** and **expressive** than guys, though there are certainly girls who aren't. While you might think of girls as chatty, they might think of you as withdrawn or quiet! *Girls are different from guys*—both in their bodies and in the way they act and think. So, until you get to know them (which could take a while!), they might seem a bit strange. Want to know what they think about boys? See Chapter 12 on the girls' side.

Why do women get CRABBY?

Women can have different ways of expressing their feelings than guys. Some guys think of this as being too emotional, but that's because a lot of guys are used to *keeping their feelings inside*. Keeping your feelings inside isn't always good, and girls tell guys this a lot. The best thing is to share what you're thinking and not to make judgments. We all get crabby at some point—it can be because we're frustrated, or we don't feel well, or we're uncomfortable, or for a lot of other reasons.

Are girls smarter or do girls just have BIGGER BRAINS?

Neither. Girls may traditionally be better at thinking in some ways, and boys may traditionally be better at thinking in other ways, *but these are generalizations*. Since girls enter puberty sooner than guys (about two years earlier) and tend to be more verbal than boys, it might *seem* like girls are smarter, but *boys and girls are about equal*. And our brains are basically the same size.

Do girls care as much as guys about the things we're talking about?

You bet! Just check out the other side of this book to see the types of questions girls are asking.

12. What Do You Do on a **Date**, Exactly?

. . . And Other Questions About Dating, Relationships, and Attractions

When do boys start to have SEXUAL THOUGHTS and is it sudden?

All boys (*and girls too*) will have sexual thoughts as they grow up—this is part of being a healthy human being and is *not bad or wrong*. It's normal. Although some guys could begin having attractions earlier, most guys experience these near the start of puberty. It won't be something you wake up suddenly having—they come gradually. It might be that a person in your class who you didn't notice before is more interesting to you now. It could be that you notice different things about people's pictures in magazines or on television. Eventually, guys "get it" that *these are thoughts of attraction* and are totally okay.

What age do boys regularly start enjoying looking at hot women in swimsuits?

When guys start to feel attractions, they start to notice other people more and notice different things about them than they used to. They might notice their faces, their body shapes, the way they move, or how they talk. You may find that you're seeing this in real people who pass by or in pictures of people in magazines. Since families and communities and cultures are different, it's important to hear from yours about what they feel comfortable with—parents can have pretty strong feelings about some of these pictures, particularly if they think they *give the wrong impression*. Ask them what they think. But, to answer your question, some guys get interested in looking at women around **puberty**, some guys later on, and some guys maybe never (see pages 61–63 to read about guys being gay).

When do SEXUAL FEELINGS stop?

Usually, sexual feelings are with you **forever**. They can change, however, as you get older. Our thoughts and attitudes change, other people change, and we gain more experience by meeting new people. Let's just say those sexual feelings will be there, but perhaps they'll be **different** than they are now.

Is it OK to have a girl as a friend?

You bet. You can be **friendly** with girls in your school, you can **play sports** or do activities with them, or you can just hang around with them like you would any guy friend. Some people (like your guy friends) might wonder if there's something romantic going on, but that might be because they don't have any girls as friends themselves and don't know that it's possible to be *friends with girls*. Just to be sure, you can even talk it over with the girl and say you like her as a friend and ask how she'd feel having a guy as a friend. Most adults have friends of the opposite gender, so it's a pretty **normal** thing. There are some cultures where this is not a usual thing, so you can also *ask your family* about this subject.

How do you TALK TO A GIRL
without flirting with them?

As a guy gets *more experience* in dealing with attraction, he learns ways to show his attraction, which some call flirting. He also learns how to interact with some girls without flirting (like with his cousin or the girl who works at the grocery store or his babysitter). This mostly comes from trial and error, but you can get some clues from *watching how other guys* around you (like guys in your family or other grown-ups) do it. Not everyone sees things in the same way, so be careful—you could think you're totally *not* flirting and someone might misinterpret it anyway. This is part of what we learn as we grow up.

What do you do on a date, exactly?

Dates can be **different** things for different people, but most think of them as a way to get to know someone in whom you're **interested**. It could be going to a dance, to the mall, or to a movie, or just *hanging out and talking*. Most families have important **rules** for dating—this is because they want to make sure you feel safe while being able to have a good time. Some rules might be that your parents need to know who you're with, where you're going, and when you're coming home. Although some teens might think their parents are being too protective or strict, a lot of teens are also happy their parents *care enough to keep them safe*.

. . . .

How old do I have to be to start dating?

Well, there's no set rule on that, except that it's the age that your **family** feels comfortable with. Sometimes guys start with a **group date**—several guys and girls doing some **activity** together—before considering the type of date with just two people. Again, your family wants you to be safe, so they might want you to *wait until they know you will be*. Some families come from cultures where dating is not done at all, and kids only get to know each other at family events. Other families come from cultures where dating is okay. Try *asking the grown-ups in your life* what rules about **dating** they had when they were teenagers.

. . . .

I have never gotten a date, will I ever?

If you're ten, eleven, twelve, or even fifteen, that's **normal**. People sometimes wait until **later** to date because they're *not ready* or because their families *aren't comfortable* with dating yet. Don't worry—there will be lots of **time** and lots of **opportunities** to date.

What is the best way to ASK THEM OUT that has the best chance of "yes"?

You probably already know the answer to that one. *Girls say they like guys* who are kind, considerate, and friendly—the same sort of things you would like in a friend of yours. Since almost all adults have *a whole bunch of experience* with this sort of thing, it might be fun to ask them what worked for them and what didn't. This type of challenge hasn't changed at all since they were dating, so perhaps you could learn from what they learned.

. . . .

What do you do if they say "no"?

This can happen. Rejection is part of *the growing-up experience*. Though sometimes it can make you feel bad, having someone say "no" will help you learn something that makes you better at asking the next time. And remember, someone might ask you out and you have the same option of saying "no" if that person *isn't right for you*. The important thing to know is that there are people out there who will say "yes" when you ask them, who will want to spend time with you and get to know you, and who will be fun to be with.

. . . .

What should you say if a really HOT GIRL asks you out?

Although in the old days guys almost always did the asking, these days there are more and more girls who might ask guys out. If this happens, you get to decide if you want to go out. *Are you ready?* Is this person right for you? Some guys wonder how to figure this out. Most guys say that it's not just how "hot" a girl is, but a lot of different factors that help him decide. Do you have things in common? Is this person fun to be with? Do you know the person enough to be able to make a decision? You can ask other guys who have gone on dates (like your dad or some other trusted adult) for *tips on what to do* and *how to manage things* if someone asks you out. Or you can just say yes, realizing that sometimes dates are really great and mostly a *learning experience*.

. . . .

How do you get a GIRLFRIEND?

Let's start with what a girlfriend is. Sometimes, guys can call a friend who is a girl a "girl friend." But usually, when guys use that word, it means someone you're dating **exclusively**—that means you're dating that girl *and no one else*. (Some families will be OK with you dating, but would prefer you to not go **steady** yet—that means *not* be with just one person all the time.) Then, if you're ready and your family's okay with it, you still have to *find someone!* If you're **friendly**, have a sense of **humor**, are considerate and a **good listener**—and if you can be yourself—it would be hard for girls *not* to like you!

. . . .

How do you keep creepy girls away and not ruin your chance with the hot ones?

Sometimes we make **judgments** about people that turn out to be wrong when we get to know them better. There's always something **good** about a person that *you can learn if you give it a try*. On the other hand, sometimes a girl could be **attracted** to you, and you might not be attracted to her. In the dating world, anybody can ask anybody for a date, and everyone has the right to say "yes" or "no." Although other boys might seem impressed if your girlfriend is beautiful or sexy, *don't get caught up in this*—there are so many great things about people besides their looks. You might find you're even more attracted to things other than a girl's looks when you get to know her.

When a guy and a girl have a relationship does the guy have to be older?

No, but because girls mature a little sooner than guys, it's more common to see girls with guys who are the same age or slightly older. As you get older, age matters less and less. It's important, though, that the difference in age isn't too great—you need to have things in common to talk about, and you should have about the same level of experience. In any case, it's not okay for a kid to date an adult because sometimes the adult takes advantage of the younger person, who is less experienced. There are laws in all states protecting kids from these situations.

How do you DUMP A GIRL?

"Dumping" someone is not a particularly nice thing to do, since it usually means ending your relationship whether or not she agrees. Anyone who is dumped generally feels really bad and rejected. This can happen to boys as well as girls. What do you do if you're dating someone and you no longer feel attracted to that person and want to stop dating them? The adult way would be to sit down and talk about how things are going for you and for her. You need to be as careful of her feelings as you would want her to be of yours. It's never easy to break up with someone, and it often makes both people feel bad, but talking it over is best.

I don't want to kiss. What do I do?

Sounds like you're not ready, which is just fine. Of course, if Aunt Tillie wants to give you a kiss on the cheek, you might have to deal with that. But romantic kissing is something people choose to do with someone they are attracted to. There are still plenty of other things you can do to show you like someone: smile at them, laugh with them, say nice things to them, do fun things with them—these are just a few but there are many, many more.

Is it normal to kiss a girl when you're 11 years old? Will it hurt you?

Some guys can feel attraction earlier than other guys. And you might have seen a romantic kiss in a movie and wondered what it's like. No, it won't hurt you, but be sure that it's okay with the girl. Also, touching someone like this gives them the signal that you're attracted to them. If you're not, maybe you'd better hold those kisses for someone *you are attracted to*.

Why do girls bother, trick, and spy on boys?

Girls generally enter puberty before boys do and progress through it a little faster. So, while boys might still be romantically uninterested in girls, girls might already be romantically interested in boys. This is why guys frequently find girls *paying attention to them* even when they've shown no indication of wanting this. When girls, and guys for that matter, begin these changes in thoughts about the opposite sex, they have to learn how to *appropriately show their feelings* and figure out what works for them. It's like dancing—it takes a while and practice to feel comfortable with some parts of growing up.

Is there a special part of you that COMES TO LIFE when you get attracted to a girl?

It certainly *can seem like that*. People have spent a lot of time and energy trying to describe the feelings they have when they become attracted to someone, but it really is one of those things you *can't quite understand* until it happens to you.

Is love meant to just keep us REPRODUCING?

There are plenty of people who fall in love with another person and never have children together. Falling in love happens when someone becomes totally attracted to another person and wants to be with them *as much as possible*. Sometimes that leads to marriage, but not always. Sometimes those couples decide to have children, *but not always*. Think about a couple who meets when they're your grandparents' age—they can fall in love just like younger people, but they might not be thinking about having kids.

What are the chances that two people will be attracted to each other? How does it happen?

If *falling in love* was like it is in the movies, you'd think it's like magic. It can happen that way in real life, but a lot of the time it takes people a while to realize they might be in love with, or even attracted to, another person. With all the people on this earth, you can bet there is someone out there who will be as attracted to you as you will be to them—and my bet is that there is more than just one. The fun is in *finding the one who is right for you*.

What's it like to FALL IN LOVE?

There's a ton of music, poetry, movies, and books written about that! Love makes some guys feel like they're going a little crazy, with all their thoughts focused on that other person. They can even stop doing things they've always liked to do. Some guys describe love as *a terrific feeling* that overwhelms you. And some guys just wonder if the feelings they have inside must be love, though they aren't sure. Love can be very different for different people. Try asking the adults in your life *how love feels to them*.

What if I don't want a wife?

Most people find that as they grow up, they really want to be with another person and get **very close** to that person. In many families, cultures, and communities, that might mean getting **married**. Hold off on that thought for now—*you're just beginning to grow up*. Lots of **changes** await you, and you might find that what you want changes too. Getting married is a choice for most people in this country—you can ask people around you who are married why they chose marriage. Then, when you're old enough, you can **decide** *if you want to get married or not*. In some countries and in some cultures, marriage is something your parents may decide for you—if you come from one of these cultures, you'll need to talk with your parents about it.

Why do some humans act homosexually?

Homosexual (or *gay*) is the word for someone who is sexually attracted to someone of his or her *own* sex. Most people are *heterosexual* (or *straight*), which means they are sexually attracted to the *other* sex. As far as we know, there have been **gay people** in every culture on earth for as long as humans have existed. One way to think about people being gay or straight is to think about people being left-handed or right-handed. Most people are right-handed, but that doesn't mean that being left-handed is wrong or bad. Does someone choose to be left-handed? *No, they were born that way*. Can you tell if someone is left-handed when he's born? No, you have to wait until he grows up enough to use one hand more than the other. Human **sexuality** is probably similar, but much more **complicated**. As far as we know, people don't choose to be sexually attracted to others of the same sex—they just *discover it when it happens*.

Some guys who are gay act **different** than guys who are straight. Other guys who are gay act just like guys who are straight. But you know what? Not all straight guys act the same, either. Being gay or straight has to do with the *person you are sexually attracted to*, not how you talk or walk or dress or act.

. . . .

When some guy is gay, is it because he gets too many of his genes from the mom (because mom likes boys so the gay guy likes boys)?

That's a very interesting thought! Scientists have tried to figure out why people are straight or gay. So far, all they know is that it has *nothing to do with hormones* (gay guys have the same amount of testosterone as straight guys), the way they were parented, or anything else that has been suggested. Perhaps one day scientists will discover why a person is gay, but in the meantime, we consider this an example of *different but normal*.

. . . .

If I am gay should I mask it?

First, sexual attractions can be confusing and complicated and some guys question their attractions and what they mean. That's OK—it can take quite a while to figure this all out. But, if you do realize you are attracted to guys, or perhaps both guys and girls, then *you should not keep it to yourself*, because that could make you feel very alone. There are many people *who do not understand* being gay, and there are many people who feel it is bad—so it's natural to want to keep it to yourself so you don't get teased, or worse. But sexuality is part of every person on earth, and it's important to recognize who you are and talk with someone about it. Sometimes talking with your parents is a good place to start, since they are the ones who care most about you. Because a lot of cultures, religions, communities, and families have strong opinions about sexual orientation, this could be a very hard subject for them to talk about. If you feel like you can't talk to your parents, maybe you can identify another trusted adult, such as a teacher or other relative, to confide in. There are also good resources online and books about sexuality to help you out. The important thing to remember is that *you are not alone*, and you are a normal and valued person, just like everyone else.

. . . .

What should I do if someone is calling me gay?

Guys sometimes call other guys names just to tease them. They make fun of the way you look or what you wear or how you talk. These people are bullies (the same stuff happens to girls; see pages 46–49 on their side). If you're being teased or bullied, that is not OK—and you should let an adult know who can help you stop it or learn ways to deal with it.

13. Why Don't Men Talk About **Feelings** and **Emotions?**

. . . And Other Questions About Friends, Feelings, and Worries

Is it better to be different or like everyone else?

That's a great question! When you're growing up, you usually want to feel included. This means you try to be interested in what others are interested in, or you pick similar clothes, or you pick the same music, *all because you want others to like you*. But as you get older, you might feel like you want to be an individual, and like you want to be treated as the unique person you are. What drives adults crazy is that teenagers can feel these two things at exactly the same time! *Even grown-ups sometimes* want to fit in and other times want to do their own thing.

What do I look like when you look at me? (What do other people see in me?)

It is totally normal for guys to wonder what other people think of them. They may ask themselves, "Am I normal?" Or, "Am I like other guys?" There are things about each of us that are the same as others—we all have two eyes, two arms, and a belly button. There are also things about each of us that might be a little *different*—we have different names, different likes and dislikes, and different appearances. *That's a good thing.* We want to feel like we **fit in**; at the same time we might *not want* to look and sound *exactly* like everyone else. Teenagers often worry about how they're seen by others. The truth is, *it's normal to wonder this*—adults do too.

Why are people shunned by others if they're not exactly alike?

All people want to be part of a group that **accepts** them and treats them well. Sometimes, people will try to make a group more **exclusive** by rejecting others from belonging to the group. They think that rejecting others will make them feel more **important**. Unfortunately, this can result in making others feel bad. Being rejected can happen to everyone at some point. That's okay—*there are plenty of other people* who would be thrilled to have you in their group.

At what age does one become bitter and hateful?

Yikes! That's quite a question! Most people are kind, loving, and full of hope and other good things. Sometimes, if someone is having a **hard time**—because of **stress**, financial issues, abuse, or unfair things done to them during their lives—they can come across as *mean* or *irritable*. Everyone has bad days, for sure, but most people are generally **good**, and they *stay that way their whole lives.*

Do your feelings for family and friends change during ages 10-20?

Our feelings can definitely change as we get older. Even though we can love our families forever, the ways we interact depend on our age and our experiences with each other. Many of us think back to friends we used to know and liked a lot but who are no longer active in our lives. We change; they change. *That's part of growing up.*

. . . .

Is it normal to fear responsibilities?

It is normal to wonder what's in store for you and even to worry about whether you'll *be able to handle it all*. But having responsibilities goes right along with having privileges—they're part of growing up. Your family, school, and community are getting you ready to handle these responsibilities when you're grown up. Try asking people in your family whether they were worried about responsibilities when they were young and *how they overcame those worries*.

. . . .

What does all the stress feel like when you are already stressed and your significant other is screaming at you?

It sounds like you might be experiencing something like this somewhere, perhaps even at home. Stress can be good or bad, depending on what type of stress it is and how much of it you have. An example of *a good type of stress* is the stress you have when you compete in a sport. You might be nervous about whether you'll win, but the competition is what makes you try harder and get better. You get the same kind of good stress when you take a test. Although few people like them, tests help you learn the subject so that you get smarter. Unfortunately, there is also bad stress. *You can experience bad stress* when you don't have enough money for basic things, or when someone is mean to you or hurting you, or when you get sick. When stresses pile up, some people have trouble dealing with them, and they act different than when things are okay. No matter what your age, it's important to talk about the stresses you're feeling with someone you can trust—someone who listens to you, and who can help you *deal with how you're feeling*. Think of three adults whom you trust—see if you can think of at least *two* besides your parents, such as another relative, a friend's parent, a coach, or a teacher. That way you'll always have someone to turn to when you need help.

. . . .

On advertisements, they put pretty women on the ad. WHAT MESSAGE ARE THEY SENDING?

Ads are made to sell you things. Good advertisers know that they need to get your attention to make you want to buy their products. So sometimes they will use something they think you'll like, and associate it with the product they're selling. For example, certain sports drinks are advertised with famous sports stars—that's so you'll think that drinking the sports drink will make you look like that athlete. Advertisers will even use things in their advertisements that have nothing to do with the products they're selling—like a pretty woman in a car commercial. They think that if you get a good feeling about the pretty woman, you'll also have a good feeling about the car and want to buy one. *Even adults fall for this*. Your question is a great thing to talk with your family about—what messages are television programs, movies, and ads sending you about growing up? Are they for real?

Who defines cool?

That's a very *hard question* to answer! **Cool** is basically defined by **groups** of people. If enough people (especially people others admire) think something is cool, the rest might go along with it and think so too. As a silly example, imagine that a famous rock group decides to wear their shorts over their heads. If you see other guys doing the same thing, you might think that wearing shorts in that way must be cool. What is cool **changes** constantly, depending on *fads and what's popular*. Every guy wants to fit in and feel important, so it's okay to want to be cool. Try asking your family how they tried to be cool at your age.

What is the point of a PORNO MOVIE?

Pornography is something in books, photographs, or videos that shows men's and women's bodies acting in a **sexual** way. Some guys take an interest in these pictures as a way to live out *the sexual thoughts they are having*. One problem with this, however, is that in many places it is illegal (for instance, to send sexual pictures through cell phones or mail to a different state; to include pictures of kids or teens; or if there are laws against sexual pictures where you live). Another **problem** with pornography is that some of the people in these pictures are treated unfairly or even hurt. Since you will inevitably run into pornography at some point, it is best to sit down with your family and ask them what they think and feel about it.

Why don't men talk about FEELINGS AND EMOTIONS?

Men don't talk as much about their feelings because they're *taught not to* in many cultures and families. In many cases, a guy's image of a man is someone who keeps his **feelings** to himself and doesn't let his emotions be **obvious** to others. This may not be the case in your family. What do you think characterizes a man? What should a man look like? How should he act? How should he behave around others? What's his role in a family or in his community? There are no easy answers to these questions, and people have very different opinions about what men should be like. This would be a great thing to talk with your family about. Maybe their opinions have changed as they got older themselves.

14. Can **Sex** Happen Accidentally?

. . . And Other Questions About Sex and Sexually Transmitted Diseases (STDs)

WHAT IS SEX, exactly?

Sex is a small word that describes a whole lot of things. When most people talk about sex, they're talking about **sexual intercourse**. Let's say that a man and a woman are sexually attracted to each other. If the guy has sexual thoughts, his penis will get erect. Then he and this woman get very **close**, skin to skin actually, and he inserts his erect penis into her vagina. If he moves it back and forth, it's just like rubbing his penis. (Remember we talked about that? See page 30.) The rubbing calls on the sperm to move from his testicles, combine with semen, and shoot out the end of his penis. He feels *a total body sensation*, called an **orgasm**.

How was sex invented?

No one "invented" or "discovered" sex—sex has always been a **part of life**. In fact, *it's how we got here*. As animals evolved, new animals came into being from sexual interactions. Sex is the way we **reproduce** ourselves.

What are some reasons people have sex? Tell me as many as you know.

People have sex to have babies. People have sex because it feels good. People have sex because it is one of the most powerful things two people can do to feel really intimate, or close to each other. There are also other reasons people have sex that might not be as good—for instance, some boys feel they need to have sex because they *think* all other boys are doing it and they don't want to be left out. We'll talk about that again later.

. . . .

When the penis goes into the vagina, is that literal?

Absolutely. The penis is basically designed for the vagina, and vice versa. If this is really surprising to you, join the club! It is for many guys when they first learn about it.

. . . .

What if your penis doesn't fit in the vagina?

Lots of people, both boys and girls, worry about this. Don't worry—it will. But remember that to be a respectful partner, you should make sure you're not hurting the other person or doing something to make that person uncomfortable. And the other person should do the same for you.

What does an orgasm feel like? PLEASE ANSWER!

It's hard to describe, but I'll try. Your heart beats faster, your muscles get tighter, you sweat, you breathe faster, and it feels pretty good. Some guys say it feels like a release, some say it feels like an explosion, and some say *it just feels great*.

. . . .

What does a girl feel during sex?

Thanks for asking that question! Some guys only think about themselves when having sex and forget that they have a partner with whom they're having this *amazing experience*. Although a girl doesn't have a penis, she does have something called a clitoris not far from the vagina that is similar—it's sensitive and it feels good when touched. Girls have orgasms too, but they sometimes need more attention and more time to experience one than a guy. That's why it's so important to talk about this stuff to learn how to be considerate of your partner. (Do you want to know more about what girls feel about sex? Flip over to Chapter 13 on the girls' side to see.)

. . . .

Do both of you (boy/girl) have to be NAKED when you have sex?

Well, that's generally the way it's done. There are many parts of our bodies that can feel good when touched romantically by another person, and *being naked* is the best way to make this happen. But you need at least to take clothes off the essential parts (the *penis* and *the vagina*) to engage in sexual/vaginal intercourse.

When do you have sex? How old? Where? When? Why?

Those are a lot of questions! Many boys wonder at what age guys start having sex. There is an answer, but it's not a specific age—a guy should have sex when he's ready. And ready means different things for different guys. For some, it means waiting until a long-term committed relationship such as marriage. For others, it means when they understand how to prevent some of the things they don't want from sex, such as an unwanted pregnancy or a sexually transmitted disease. It doesn't make sense to just do what your friends are doing, since guys tend to exaggerate about this stuff. Listening to others, you might think that you're the only one who hasn't had sex yet—*not true*. Lots of guys wait because they feel they're not ready. The important thing to remember is that having sex is a choice you make, and only when you're ready. Oh, and don't forget your partner needs to feel ready too!

Is there a sign that tells you that you are ready to have sex?

Not that I can think of, except the feeling that you might be ready, and knowing that the other person is also ready. That's *equally important*.

Will sex affect my daily life?

Some boys in their teens spend a lot of time thinking about sex. But there are a lot of other things to do as well—school, homework, sports, hobbies, spending time with family, eating, hanging out, etc. Make sure you leave time for all that other stuff—*sex will come when you are ready*.

What makes a man think that sex is disgusting when they are young but when they get older they like sex?

During puberty, your brain changes, just like your body. Testosterone causes new thoughts and desires to come your way, and as you grow up, you experience a ton of things that are new to you. A year from now, you could have *a totally different attitude* about something that you find gross now. Or it might take ten years for your opinions to change. That's okay—each guy takes his own time to get comfortable with all these changes.

. . . .

Can sex happen accidentally?

No. Sex is something one chooses to do. Sometimes when a guy does something that he later feels he shouldn't have, he might try to use the excuse that it was "accidental." But we all know it *doesn't work like that*.

. . . .

Why do people have sex if they don't want a baby?

People have sex because it feels good and because it makes them feel really close to each other in their relationship. But, since there's a chance sex can result in getting pregnant, both partners have to understand this. If you and your partner are not ready to be parents, then you both need to think ahead to keep this from happening. (See pages 79–80 on the girls' side for more information on preventing unwanted pregnancy.)

What do you do other than penis into vagina when you have sex?

Sex is a *little* word with a *lot* of meanings. You can **feel** sexual without *doing* anything. To some people, hugging and holding hands can be really sexual. Our **bodies** have lots of places that can make us feel sexual—experiencing sex with another person means **exploring** what's sexual for you and what's sexual for them. For a lot of guys, getting your first **romantic kiss** can give you a thrill down your spine—*that's being sexual too*.

How do guys know how to have sex?

Knowing how to have sex is part of **being ready**. You can read about it in a trusted book (like this one!), you can learn about it in school, you can talk with your parents about it, and you can learn from your sexual partner when you talk things through. But like any new **experience**, it can be a little nerve-racking when you're not sure what you're doing—that's true for everyone.

My friend thinks that when you KISS the woman gets pregnant. Is that true?

No, just **kissing** can't possibly lead to pregnancy. A woman gets pregnant when a sperm gets to her egg. Her eggs are down in her **reproductive system** (see illustrations on page 31 on the girls' side), so that's where a guy's sperm has to go to get her **pregnant**. There have been many, many myths over the centuries about how someone gets pregnant. But now you *know how it really happens*, so when a friend comes up to you and says, "I heard a girl can get pregnant when a boy shakes her hand or winks at her," you can set him straight.

What does a date have to do with sex?

Some guys get confused and think a date is the same thing as having sex. Not true. A date is when two people **spend time** together. A date could be getting a snack at a restaurant, watching a movie, taking a walk together, or even just hanging out and talking. On the other hand, sometimes guys think a date is the right **opportunity** to have sex and may be hoping for it since they might be alone with the person they're dating. (See Chapter 12 for more on dating.)

. . . .

Why do people want to pretend to have sex?

Some boys think it will **impress** other guys to tell them they've had sex so other guys will like them, respect them, or think they're cool. It's just like **bragging** in any other way—like telling others you've got superpowers or climbed Mount Everest blindfolded. Since *it's normal* to want to feel **important** and be included, some guys resort to bragging because they think it's the only way to get the positive attention they want. But weirdly, the more a guy brags, the less other guys want to be around him. If a guy announces to everyone that he's had sex, you might think of him as grown-up, or you might think of him as foolish if he wasn't really ready.

. . . .

How does it work from being boyfriend-girlfriend to sex?

Many, many couples decide to go steady but wait on having sex until they're **ready**. Also, many families, faiths, cultures, and communities have fairly strong feelings about when people should have sex, or even go steady. Many teens decide that being ready is very important to them too, and hold off on having sex. In any case, it's not just you who has to be ready—it's **both** of you. You can do a million things with someone you care about—and show you really care about them—without having sex with them.

When people get married, do they have sex every day?

No, most married people don't have sex every day. Sex is a very special thing people share with each other—*it takes time and caring*. People have to work, sleep, eat, take care of the kids, and do other things they like to do. Sometimes it's hard to find time to fit sex in!

. . . .

What would I do if I WAS FORCED to have sex and I didn't want to?!

Sex should only happen if both people are ready. If one person is not ready and the other person forces them to have sex, then it's seriously bad. It's not only hurtful and disrespectful, but it's also illegal. It doesn't matter if you're forced or doing the forcing—both are wrong. And making someone have sex doesn't just happen physically. If someone says "no" to sex and the other person pushes and pushes until the other person just gives in, then that is forcing too. Some guys think that a girl is supposed to say "no" when first asked to have sex, even if she really wants to. But "no" means "no." So, what can *you* do if someone is pressuring you to have sex and you're not ready? You could simply say no. If you like the person but you're not ready, you could say, "I'm just not ready for that, but we can still do other things together." Or, if the person is hurting you, you can *tell a trusted adult* or the authorities. *No one* should have sex if they are not ready.

How do you get a girl to have sex with you without forcing them?

If she's not ready, then *sex doesn't happen*. You might ask her what **ready** is for her. Or you might just figure out **other things** to do together that show you **care** about her. You could give her a gift, play video games together, do homework together, talk on the phone, go to her house to meet her family, hang out together, meet her friends, play sports with her, take a walk, see a movie, or just talk with her. I bet you can think of many more things too.

. . . .

What if I did not want to have sex and yet I want to have kids?

Well, you certainly could **adopt** children as an alternative to having them yourself. But **wait** on that decision until you're older. You might just *change your mind*.

. . . .

Do you have to do it?

You mean sex? **No**. Some guys choose never to have sex, for various reasons. Sex is a **choice**—except when it is forced and then it's wrong. Most guys in the world choose to have sex, however. Why? There are many reasons. To be *close to someone*, to **experience** it, and to be a dad are just a few.

What disease can you get from having sex that you CAN'T DIE FROM?

Sometimes we can get diseases that make us sick. For example, you can get a cold if another kid with a cold coughs or sneezes in your direction. There are other diseases that can come from sexual contact with another person—these are called sexually transmitted diseases, or STDs. There are a whole bunch of them. Some are caused by viruses, some by bacteria, and some by other things. Some STDs (like *chlamydia*) can be cured by taking medicine; some can be prevented by having a vaccine but not cured once you have them, like human papillomavirus (HPV); while others can be extremely serious and have no cure, like human immunodeficiency virus (HIV)—the virus that causes acquired immunodeficiency syndrome (AIDS). The only totally effective way—absolutely, without question—to avoid ever getting an STD is to never have sex with anyone. *Can you choose that?* Yes, you can. But as we discussed before, there would be some things you'd be missing out on, such as fathering a child of your own some day. So, there are precautions you can take to avoid getting one of these diseases—staying with one sexual partner, using condoms, getting a vaccine to prevent some STDs, getting you and your partner tested before having sex—but there is always some risk when one chooses to have sex.

. . . .

How many girls out of a hundred have SEXUAL DISEASES?

Enough people have STDs that you need to think about it *before having sex.* Girl or guy, you *can't tell* by looking at someone if they have an STD. Most of the diseases can be silent—meaning you may have the disease but have no symptoms. Many people who have an STD have no idea that they have it. So, how can you know? You can get tested—at your doctor's office or at a special clinic.

Tests could include an exam and perhaps a urine test or a blood test. Are the tests perfect? Well, not entirely, but they're really, really good at helping you know if you have an STD.

. . . .

What is AIDS? How do you get it? Did they have it when you were growing up?

Acquired immune deficiency syndrome, or AIDS, is a disease caused by a virus called human immunodeficiency virus, or HIV. Like most viruses, HIV is incurable, though we've recently discovered some medicines that can mostly control it—but someone with HIV would have to take these drugs for the rest of his or her life. HIV damages your immune system, which protects you from infections and from cancers. So people with AIDS can get very sick and die from these things. When someone just gets HIV, they usually have no clue that the virus is working inside them—there are no particular symptoms—so the only way to know is to take a test. The test is easy and great at telling someone if they have HIV or not. Once the virus stays around for a while, it can progress to the disease AIDS, which can make a person very sick.

You can get HIV by having sexual contact with someone who has the virus, even if they don't seem sick at all. You can also get it by getting someone else's blood in your body, like through a blood transfusion. (Don't worry—the blood you would get in a hospital in the United States is checked completely and is extremely safe.) Also, people who use certain drugs that require injection by needle, such as heroin, can get the virus by sharing someone else's needles.

Was AIDS around when I was young? Not that we knew of, but it probably came from another country where it only affected a few people. AIDS became big news when it spread to many people all over the world.

If you have a CONDO, can you still get HIV?

I think you mean a condom! A condom is made of latex or plastic, looks like a water balloon, and fits over a guy's penis before he has sex with someone. Guys use it to prevent an STD (either getting one or giving one) and to prevent sexual partners from getting pregnant. You can buy condoms of all types at drugstores or convenience stores. To prevent STDs or pregnancy, a guy has to use one every time he has sex, not just occasionally, and put it on his erect penis before it gets close to his sexual partner. When he ejaculates (when sperm come out), the condom catches his sperm and semen, which prevents their contact with his sexual partner. *Does it work perfectly?* Well, it works really well for some diseases, like HIV, if used properly. For other diseases that can be elsewhere on your body other than your penis, such as crabs (little insects that can be anywhere on your skin), condoms aren't as effective. The biggest reason condoms might not work is that guys don't use them properly—it's totally okay to ask your parent or another trusted adult how to use a condom the right way (since the instructions are not on the condom wrapper).

. . . .

How does it feel to wear a condom?

It feels *like a tight piece of skin* over your penis. Most condoms are made so that guys still feel everything they would without one, but a guy might want to try different brands to see which works best for him. Some guys (and women!) have an allergy to the latex, so they make non-latex condoms also. You might hear guys tell you they don't like how the condom feels, but getting an STD or making some-one pregnant *can feel a lot worse!*

How can a girl get pregnant and still prevent getting an STD?

Great question! You might be wondering how a couple that tries to prevent STDs by having the guy use a condom can *make a baby* if they want to. The simple answer is: you can't get pregnant if you use a condom—that same condom that keeps diseases from spreading also keeps the sperm from the egg. But there is a way to prevent STDs without preventing pregnancy—have sex with only **one partner**, who also has never had sex with anyone but you. That way, neither of you could have picked up an STD to give to the other. This is one reason why some people choose to wait to have sex until they are in a long-term **relationship**, such as marriage. Still another option is for each of you to **get tested** for STDs before having sex together. The tests aren't perfect, but they are really good at **preventing** STDs. Both people need to be sexual with that one person only, since once they have sex with someone else, there's the risk of getting an STD. It takes two people to think through how to avoid getting or passing STDs.

But what if you don't want to make someone pregnant right now, either? Are there other ways to keep from getting pregnant if a couple doesn't want it? Sure! Besides having the guy use a **condom**, you can choose not to have sexual intercourse, there are various hormones the woman can take, there's spermicide that kills sperm, there are **devices** a woman can use to block her cervix—and more. Go to page 80 on the girls' side to learn more about all that.

15. Is a **Pregnant** Man Possible?

. . . And Other Questions About Pregnancy and Childbirth

If you are a boy, and you're having sex with a girl, will the girl always have a baby?

So, now that we've talked about sexual intercourse, let's talk about **pregnancy**. If a guy ejaculates when his penis is inside a woman's vagina, then millions of sperm are released inside her, right near her *cervix*, or the entrance to her uterus (see the picture on page 31 on the girls' side). Since **sperm** don't really know where to go, they will *swim in all directions*, but lots of them will happen to swim through a tiny hole in the cervix, through the uterus, and up into the fallopian tubes. If there's an egg already being moved down one of these tubes, then the first sperm to get to the **egg** combines with it to start a pregnancy. If there is no egg in the tube at the time, then the sperm simply die and are eliminated by the woman's body.

Once a single sperm combines with an egg, the egg puts a wall around itself, which prevents any more sperm from getting in. In the meantime, the chromosomes from the egg (which come from the mom) and those from the sperm (which come from the dad) combine. Right away, the cells start multiplying as a new baby starts to form. This **zygote**, or combined egg and sperm, gets moved down to the uterus, where it sticks to the uterine wall, which has been preparing for it. And it **grows** and **grows**.

About **nine months** later, the baby is done growing and is ready to come out. He or she sends a message to the uterus (a strong muscle that stretches really big to hold the growing baby), which then contracts and pushes the baby down. The tiny hole in the cervix has to stretch to let the baby's head (which usually comes first) through. *Ouch!* Both the contractions of the uterus and the stretching of the hole in the cervix hurt a lot—like a muscle cramp in your leg but much worse. This is why they call it *labor pain*. Finally, a **baby** gets pushed out through the vagina and is born!

. . . .

I heard I was TOO BIG to be born the usual way. So, how did that work?

Most babies are born through the **vagina**, with their heads coming through first. Some are turned around, with their butt coming first. Some babies can be **too big** to fit through, no matter how hard the mom is trying to push them out. In these cases, the doctor will anesthetize the mom (put her to sleep or numb her up) and make a **cut** down low in her belly, right into the uterus, and take the baby out that way. Then the mom gets sewn back up. This is called a caesarian section or **C-section**.

. . . .

I've heard that if you have sex on a certain day it will affect whether you have a BOY or GIRL.

Throughout history, people have wondered what determines the **gender** of a baby—whether it will be a boy or a girl. Generally, it has **nothing** to do with the day you have sex, what you eat, what you're thinking, or what you're wearing before you have sex. Half of the dad's sperm carry an "X" chromosome and half carry the "Y" chromosome. Whichever **sperm** happens to get to the egg first *determines which sex the baby will be*. The mom's egg has nothing to do with the gender of the baby, since all eggs have the "X" chromosome. If a "Y"-carrying sperm combines with an egg, it makes an "XY," which will be a boy. If an "X"-carrying sperm combines with an egg, then it's a girl, or "XX."

. . . .

What does it mean when my mom tells me she "tied the knot" so she won't have any more kids?

That means your mom asked a surgeon to cut her fallopian tubes (which carry the egg to the uterus and the sperm to the egg) and tie off the ends. Women can choose to do this to make sure they can *never get pregnant* if they don't want any more babies. There are other ways to keep from getting pregnant—this is called contraception (you can learn more on pages 79–80 on the girls' side). If someone doesn't want to be pregnant, then both people in the relationship need to think about how to prevent it.

. . . .

When a sperm and an egg meet and make a baby, is it the 1st time it works or do you do it many times?

Since a woman's egg ripens *only once a month* and a baby can only start in the fallopian tube, there is really only about one week out of every month when a woman can get pregnant. If a woman has sex during this week then she could get pregnant, but some couples have to have sex several times before the woman gets pregnant. If a couple has sex at other times when there isn't an egg in the tube, then the woman won't get pregnant. Also, because some women don't know exactly when the egg is going to start its trip into the fallopian tube, relying on just not having sex during that fertile week is not a dependable way to prevent pregnancy.

Can a woman give birth without having sex?

Generally speaking, a woman can't give birth without having sex, since *having sex is the main way of getting pregnant*. In modern times, however, scientists have discovered that it's possible for doctors to remove an egg surgically from the mom's ovary, get some sperm from the dad, and combine them in the laboratory. Then this zygote, or combination of egg and sperm, is placed back into the mom's uterus to grow into a baby. This process is called artificial insemination, and some couples might choose to do this if they are having trouble getting pregnant the traditional way.

. . . .

How do girls know that they're PREGNANT?

Some women know that they're pregnant as soon as their periods stop happening (see Chapter 7 on the girls' side for lots more details about periods). Women don't have bleeding, or periods, when they're pregnant because the uterus is holding on to its lining to start growing the baby. When a woman is pregnant, she can also have other symptoms that come from the pregnancy hormones her body makes—symptoms like an upset stomach or a different appetite. Also, most women feel their bellies grow as the uterus gets larger. But if it's really early in the pregnancy, a woman may do a simple urine test that can tell her she's pregnant even before she feels anything.

. . . .

Can a baby come out the butt?

No, never. Babies are born through a woman's vagina, which is a different area (see the picture on page 31 on the girls' side). For more on how the girl's reproductive system works, see Chapter 7 on the girls' side.

If a guy has masturbated in a public toilet and doesn't flush it, and then a girl drops an egg in the toilet, and the sperm is still alive, will a baby grow in the toilet?

Sperm need special conditions to stay alive—they need to be kept moist and close to body temperature. If sperm left your body and ended up on a toilet seat, they'd die pretty quickly. And eggs can generally only get fertilized when they're in the fallopian tube (except in the case of artificial insemination; see page 87 for more about this). So by the time an egg passes through a woman's vagina, it's too late for it to get fertilized. Plus, a baby needs a uterus to develop and grow. So there are *lots of reasons* why this can't possibly happen!

. . . .

Would the size of a woman's egg affect the height of the child?

No, eggs are all the same size and look about the same. But inside, each one carries a slightly different set of the mom's genes. Each one brings a message about how tall the baby should be. Of course, so do the dad's sperm. Guys tend to take after their dads a little more than their moms, and guys tend to be taller than women, but *both the egg and the sperm* are important in determining exactly how tall a baby will grow to be.

. . . .

Is a boy's birth different from a girl's?

No, they look exactly the same. Sometimes the mom (and the dad, if he's there at the time) has to wait until a doctor or nurse takes a look at the baby to know which it is. If there's a little penis there, it's a boy! If not, it's a girl!

Where does the UMBILICAL CORD come from?

Right after an egg and a sperm get together, the special lining of the uterus is all that's needed to give the growing baby what it needs for nutrition. But as the baby gets bigger, the uterine lining forms into a special organ called a *placenta*, which connects itself to the baby at its belly button through a long cord-like thing, which is called the umbilical cord. The umbilical cord *carries food and oxygen* from the mom to the growing baby—just like a lifeline takes oxygen to an astronaut when he or she is doing a space walk—and then takes waste from the baby and returns it to the mom to get rid of. When a baby is born, that connection isn't needed anymore since the baby will breathe on its own and get nutrition in other ways, so the umbilical cord gets cut, leaving the baby with a belly button to remember it by.

Where do other sperm go after 1 gets chosen to be the baby? If another sperm gets in, will that make twins?

Once a single sperm gets into an egg, another sperm cannot. It just can't happen, because that would create too many genes to make a person. (For more on twins, see page 84 on the girls' side.) Meanwhile, any extra sperm around get destroyed by the woman's body.

Is a PREGNANT MAN possible?

No, you have to be born with a uterus to get pregnant, which means you have to be biologically female. What makes a man a man is that he has a different *reproductive system*, which makes sperm to give to a woman to make a child. Sometimes you might read about weird things that happen out there in the world—be careful what you believe until you can figure out the whole story.

Is it possible for a GAY COUPLE to have a baby?

Since guys don't have what it takes to grow babies (no ovaries, no eggs, and no uterus), they can't have a baby the usual way. A gay male couple has a few choices—they can adopt a baby (there are lots of babies who need a good home) or one of them can father a child with a woman by donating sperm. If the gay couple is two women, they can also adopt or one of them can get pregnant with sperm from a donor guy.

. . . .

So, in the end, I'm JUST A SPERM, right?

You are way, way more than a sperm. You are a boy growing up—that means you are an amazing human being who is embarking on an exciting expedition to discover life. You are *a thinking, feeling guy*. You are a son, grandson, friend, student, perhaps a brother or a scholar, and for sure a regular, normal guy. You will become a man—*wow, imagine that*. You will notice changes in yourself and changes all around you as you grow. You'll have the opportunity to make a zillion choices about where you want to go and what you want to do. And, if you choose, you can be a father yourself one day and perhaps help your son (or daughter) to successfully complete this same growing-up trip that you're going through right now.

FLIP THIS BOOK TO READ THE GIRLS' SIDE!

Printed in China

Published by Sasquatch Books
17 16 15 14 13 12   9 8 7 6 5 4 3 2 1

Cover and interior illustrations: Lia Cerizo
Cover design: Lia Cerizo and Anna Goldstein
Interior design and composition: Anna Goldstein

Library of Congress Cataloging-in-Publication Data is available.

ISBN-13: 978-1-57061-739-3
ISBN-10: 1-57061-739-2

Sasquatch Books
1904 3rd Avenue, Suite 710
Seattle, WA 98101
(206) 467-4300
www.sasquatchbooks.com
custserv@sasquatchbooks.com

GIRLS

Will Puberty Last my Whole Life?

REAL Answers to REAL Questions from Preteens About Body Changes, Sex, and Other Growing-Up Stuff

. . . .

Julie Metzger, RN, MN, and Robert Lehman, MD

Illustrated by Lia Cerizo

SASQUATCH BOOKS
SEATTLE

Contents

Introduction

Welcome to the book of questions on puberty, sex, and other growing-up stuff asked by preteen girls (and boys too—flip the book over to see the other side!).

Who is asking these questions, you might ask? Every single question in this book has been written on a note card by someone *just like you.* For more than twenty years Julie Metzger (me) has been talking with girls and their moms, and Rob Lehman with boys and their dads, in a class by Great Conversations on important ideas about growing up. (Wow! That is a *lot* of classes and a *lot* of questions!)

In our classes we talk about what happens as our bodies change from girls to adult women (a process called puberty), everything that happens to boys' bodies during puberty (wow, *really?*), about how we make decisions in friendships and relationships, and all about sex, sexuality, and babies. In our classes we invite the girls, mostly ten to twelve years old, to ask a question on a note card so we can answer them for the whole group—and we've saved every one of those questions! *This book is a collection* of some of the questions that are asked the most, some of our favorites sprinkled in, and some that really helped everyone understand what is on the minds of preteens as they are growing up.

Even though all these questions are asked by preteens, we hope you will share some of the questions and answers with your parents, teachers, or anyone else interested in what might be on *your* mind and the minds of other preteens. We know that parents and other trusted adults in your life are some of the most important resources you have—and they *want* this whole growing-up thing to go well for you! Our answers are not meant to tell the whole story or be the final word—*just the opposite.* We hope you'll feel comfortable talking further about some of these subjects with those adults who are close to you—that's the whole idea of having Great Conversations!

Our most grateful thanks to all the girls (and boys!) who participated in our classes, and were **brave** enough to submit a question and **curious** enough to keep asking questions on subjects that were obviously important to them.

And thanks to our colleagues who reviewed the material to keep us honest, the kids who reviewed the material to keep us developmentally on-target, and our **friends and families** who made sure it stayed interesting.

And thanks most of all to my parents, Jerry and PR, for their lifetime of advocacy for me and for so many others; to Michael for his enduring love; and to Peter, Katie, and Emma for their daily inspiration.

Julie

JULIE GIESY METZGER, RN, MN

Julie Metzger, RN, MN, has worked for more than twenty years with families of preteens and teens on topics of puberty, sexuality, and decision making. Bringing a wealth of knowledge from her experiences, Metzger is a well-respected and popular speaker on a wide range of parenting issues, has worked in many capacities as a nurse consultant, and is the parent of three young adults. She has shared her program Heart to Heart For Girls Only with tens of thousands of families at Seattle Children's Hospital, Lucile Packard Children's Hospital at the Stanford Medical Center, and throughout the Puget Sound region. Julie has also written and presented health curricula on decision making and friendships for middle and high school students and advocated for adolescents and families in the community through Great Conversations. For more information on classes, programs, and other resources, visit GreatConversations.com.

great **conversations**
about growing up. together.

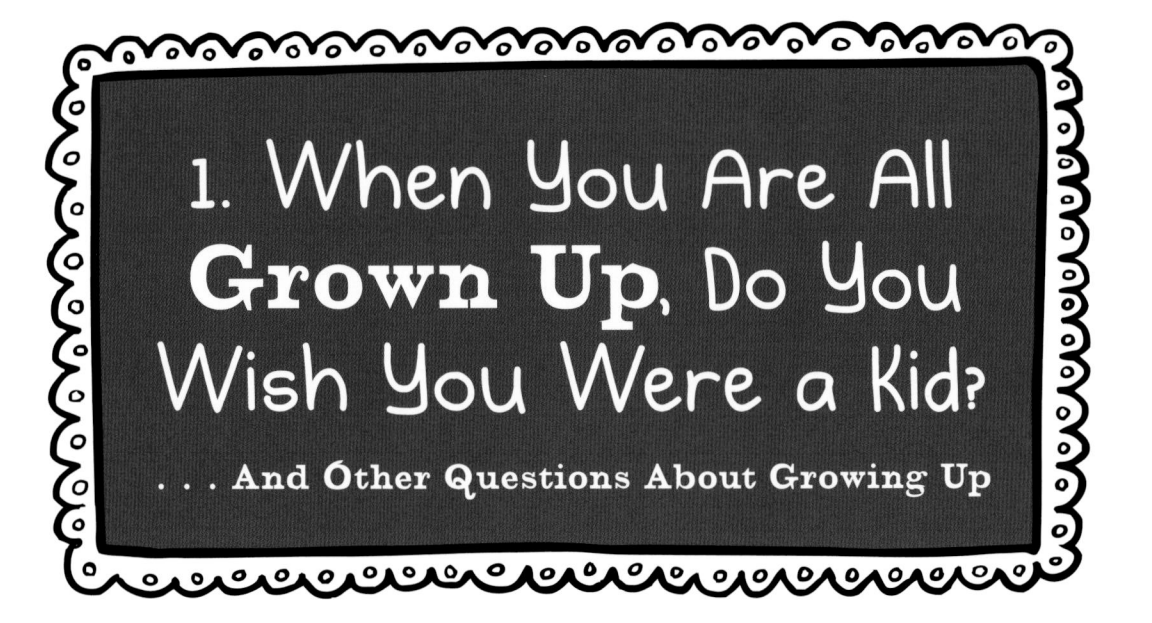

1. When You Are All Grown Up, Do You Wish You Were a Kid?

. . . And Other Questions About Growing Up

What is the POINT of puberty?

Puberty describes the process of your body **changing** *from a girl's into a* **woman's.** The entire transformation takes several years, and when it is finished, you pretty much look like a **grown-up.** The "point" of puberty is to make it possible for girls' bodies to function like women's, including the ability to be pregnant and feed a baby.

. . . .

Do ALL GIRLS have puberty?

Yes—although each girl's experience will be both the **similar** and **different** from other girls. Some girls start puberty earlier, some finish later, but most girls experience the basics, including growing *taller*, gaining weight, *growing breasts*, getting pimples and body odor, growing hair in new and interesting places, and having periods. *Believe it or not*, even boys have puberty! (To learn more about what is the same and different about boys in puberty, flip this book over and check out the questions boys have in Chapter 1.)

When will all this happen for me?

Although *puberty for girls* often starts with an increase in height and weight, lots of girls don't notice that puberty has begun since they have been busy *growing their whole lives!* Many girls first notice they have started puberty when they begin to develop breasts—this is the first *new* body change of puberty for girls (for much more about breasts, turn to page 20). Girls typically *start* puberty sometime between the ages of eight and eleven. It's not uncommon for girls to begin puberty up to *two years* before boys!

The timing of puberty is greatly influenced by heredity. We tend to follow the growth patterns of other people who are genetically linked to us. In addition to our birth parents sharing genetic messages of eye and hair color, they also pass along *how fast or slow puberty happens*, the size of our breasts, our height and shape, and even how early our period starts.

. . . .

What if you want to talk about stuff but you are TOO SHY?

Talking about puberty can sometimes feel awkward because you are mentioning body parts that are usually hidden, and seeing changes to your body that are new and sometimes unfamiliar. Plus, you *don't* hear people talking about it in everyday conversations at the dinner table or the bus stop: "Hey—your puberty is really looking great!" However, there are three guarantees about puberty that might make things easier. First, *everyone grows up*, so you are not alone. Second, *lots of people* are also shy and uncertain about how to talk about everything to do with puberty, so you are not alone on this either. Third, a lot of people—your parents, teachers, friends, sisters, and grandparents—want the whole puberty experience to go well for you and *would love to help you out*.

What BODY PART does puberty start at?

The whole process of puberty starts in your brain in a small gland called the pituitary. The pituitary gland sends a message to your ovaries that signals your body to begin growing and changing. (Wonder where your pituitary gland and ovaries are hanging out? Check out the picture on page 4 to see.) Your ovaries then send hormones (chemicals that travel around in your blood) to alert the rest of your body to start all of these changes. The primary hormone of puberty for girls is called estrogen, but progesterone and a small amount of testosterone also help out with all of the changes of puberty.

. . . .

What will "GROWING UP" do to my future? Am I really ready to have all these changes in my life, at the age of 10?

"Growing up" is the work of becoming a grown-up. Your body and brain are changing to prepare you for doing all sorts of things in the future—like driving a car, having a baby, working at a job, buying groceries, being in love, reaching for the cookie jar . . . you get the idea! The word *puberty* describes how your *body* grows from a girl's body to a woman's body, and the word "adolescence" describes how your *brain* changes to make adult decisions and have adult relationships. Put together, growing up *takes many years*, so don't worry—you've got some time before you are officially grown-up!

. . . .

Will I still have puberty when I am 50?

Puberty is officially over when your body stops growing. So most girls finish puberty when they're teenagers. However, our bodies continue to change in interesting ways *our whole lives*.

WHAT'S HAPPENING TO ME?

Pituitary
Gland
(near your brain)

Pimples

Underarm Hair

Breasts

Broadening
Hips

Uterus

Fallopian
Tubes

Vagina

Ovaries

Pubic
Hair

How will going through puberty affect my SOCCER GAME?

Your new **height** and **weight** might make you *faster or slower* on the field; you might need bigger shoes and a bigger uniform; or you might need to pack a tampon or pad in your duffel bag (see Chapter 7 for more on that!). But you can still be a soccer **superstar** while you're going through puberty.

. . . .

Is it important to have a door to your room during puberty?

When you are *going through puberty*, it can sometimes feel like your whole body is in a construction zone as it transforms into an adult shape and size. That can make you feel more self-conscious and make you want more **privacy**. Having a **place** where you can **think through** things on your own without interruptions can be helpful. As important as all of this is, it's not a requirement for someone in puberty to have her own door or even her own room. However, that doesn't mean that you can't *look for safe places* where you can be by yourself. You might find it helpful to keep a journal where you can write down your experiences and feelings.

. . . .

What do you say when a friend asks you a question about puberty and their mom hasn't told them anything about it? Do you answer?

When someone asks you a question, it means they **trust** you for information, and they are hoping that you will answer without teasing them or making them feel stupid or silly. **Acknowledging** someone's curiosity and interest is the first place to start. Then give them a brief answer if you feel you know what to say. Finish with an idea of where they could find more **information**. Something like this: "That's a great question—*I had that same one*. When someone bumps into me or hugs me too

tight *my breasts really hurt*, almost like a bruise. It has something to do with them growing. I have a book that is helpful. Want to borrow it?"

. . . .

Does puberty make you TIRED?

How we *take care of our bodies* can impact how they grow during puberty. With so much happening, our bodies need the fuel from healthy food and good sleep in order to grow well. While your body is sleeping, chemicals in your brain and bloodstream that influence your growth are going to work—your body and your brain need sleep to do the work of growing. It is entirely typical for someone going through puberty to need about nine hours of sleep. Many girls going through puberty feel tired from all of that growing *plus* all of the things they do all day—like hanging with friends and riding bikes and working on math problems!

. . . .

Will I change my ATTITUDE when I go through puberty and do something like smoke or get tattoos?

While our bodies are going through puberty, our brains are undergoing changes too. In fact, our brains continue to mature even after our bodies have finished puberty. Your body might be finished growing sometime in high school, but your brain will continue the work of wiring itself for making adult decisions into your early twenties. Making decisions about how to care for our bodies is part of growing up. There is no reason that you ever need to say "yes" to things that are dangerous to your health, like smoking, or permanent, like tattoos. *Waiting until your brain matures* and you can weigh the consequences of your choices is a great option.

When you are all "grown up," do you wish you were a kid?

I know that some kids wish they were adults at times and some adults wish they were kids at times—but I think people are generally **happiest** when they like being who they are right then and there.

. . . .

Why are there so many MEAN WORDS about a woman's body parts?

I know it sounds odd, but when people feel something is **mysterious**, sacred, or very important, they sometimes try to *diminish the idea* by giving it a mean name. I think they feel it shrinks the big idea down to a smaller idea that they are more comfortable with, and that they can laugh at instead of talk about. Using mean words for women's body parts happens when people **don't know** quite what to do with the mystery or **importance** of our bodies. And sometimes people use those words because they hear them being used by others, and they think that if they say the same things, they'll be more cool or interesting. Most commonly, you hear nicknames or mean words about the body parts that are uniquely female—like "boobs" or "tits" instead of "breasts." There are nicknames for boys' body parts too. People generally don't make up mean words about the body parts we all share. As people mature and see their own and each other's bodies as worthy of **care** and **honor**, their words change to reflect their understanding.

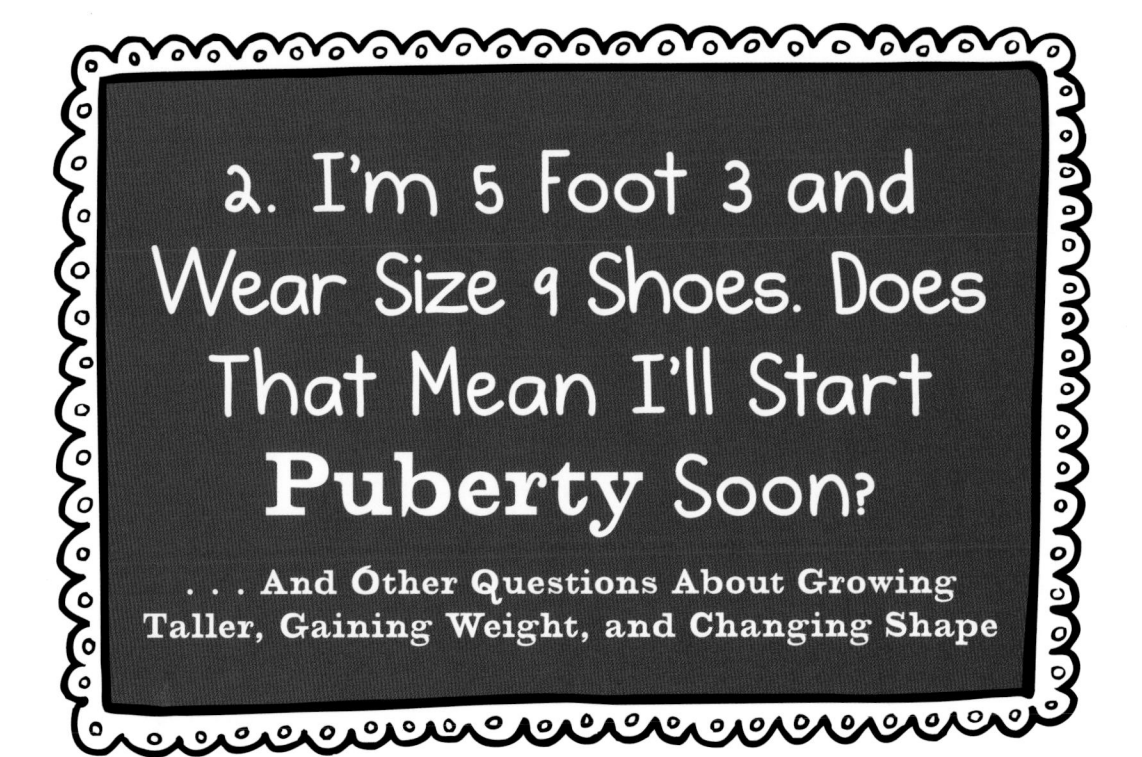

2. I'm 5 Foot 3 and Wear Size 9 Shoes. Does That Mean I'll Start **Puberty** Soon?

. . . And Other Questions About Growing Taller, Gaining Weight, and Changing Shape

What is the best kind of food to eat when in puberty?

Eating **healthy food** gives your body what it needs to get *taller and stronger*. You need enough calories and fuel to think well, write poetry, study, and run plays on the basketball court. Calcium and protein fuel bone and muscle development, iron builds healthy blood cells, while fruits, vegetables, and grains give your body vitamins and minerals to stay healthy and give you **energy**.

In particular, girls in puberty need to get enough calcium in their diets. When you are in puberty, your body absorbs **calcium** better than it does when you're an adult, so it's important to make certain you have enough calcium now in order to have healthy **bones** later. Calcium can be found in milk products like yogurt, cheese, and, well, milk; in dark green vegetables like broccoli and spinach; and in other foods like salmon.

If my mom is 5 foot 4 inches tall and my dad is 5 foot 8 inches tall and I am very small for my age and I am in the 6th grade, HOW TALL AM I GOING TO BE?

How tall you become depends a lot on how tall other members of your birth **family** are—you will most likely be close to the height of the other people to whom you are genetically connected. A girl between the ages of eight and thirteen can grow anywhere from two to ten **inches** during puberty. But how tall will you be **exactly?** *That's going to be a surprise.*

. . . .

What if I have not gained weight or grown for a year?

Growing taller and *gaining weight* happens **gradually**—and not always as fast or as evenly as we would like. Sometimes someone grows a lot, then doesn't seem to grow as much for a while, and then grows really quickly again. It is also possible that you are **growing**, but it doesn't seem like it because your friends are growing more quickly right now. *But your body is doing its work!*

. . . .

I'm 5 foot 3 inches tall and wear size 9 shoes. Does that mean I'll START PUBERTY soon?

There isn't a certain height, weight, or shoe size that means you are officially starting puberty. However, a significant **change** in height and/or weight (called a **growth spurt**) and an increase in shoe size is one of the first signs that a girl is starting puberty. A growth spurt can look very different for different people, and *sometimes people don't even notice!* Perhaps one girl grows an inch every year and then suddenly grows four inches taller in one year. Another girl might grow a quarter

of an inch every year and now grows one whole inch over the same amount of time. Both girls grew four times more than they have ever grown in a single year. Two girls, two different amounts of growth, and yet both girls are in a growth spurt and both *may be starting puberty.*

. . . .

I've gotten fat this year. Will it GO AWAY?

Gaining weight is an essential part of puberty. If we grew taller without putting on any weight, then we'd eventually need special cement shoes to keep our feet on the ground during windstorms! Our bodies need to add weight and *healthy amounts of body fat* to work well and to grow the way they are meant to during puberty. Body fat stores vitamins that we need to stay healthy; protects some of our organs, like our livers and stomachs; is a major building block of our brains; and is a part of every body cell.

Girls between the ages of eight and thirteen might gain anywhere from fifteen to fifty-five pounds during puberty. And healthy girls during puberty add about twice as much fat to their bodies as healthy boys do—it's an expected and necessary part of their body's development. It is totally possible for someone to grow tall and *then* put on weight—and it is totally possible to put on weight and *then* get taller. Read on for more advice about gaining healthy weight during puberty.

. . . .

Why do your thighs get big?

As a girl's hormones increase in puberty, she gains weight. Her body shape also changes—her hips and thighs broaden, and her breasts grow. It is typical for a girl to add fat to her body around her hips and thighs; this fat prepares her body for *a possible pregnancy* in the future. Women who are pregnant use the extra fat stores as energy and fuel throughout pregnancy and while they are nursing babies. In healthy-weight females, fat does not increase significantly after a woman is in her early twenties.

At what age should a girl start to worry about LOSING WEIGHT?

Gaining weight is part of what you can expect in puberty (check out the question on page 10 on "getting fat") since your body is growing and changing shape, and you're storing more fat on your body. As an adult woman, your body needs to grow and develop in healthy ways, which means weighing the right amount to give your body the *fuel it needs to work well*. Sometimes it can seem like women are always talking about losing weight—about being dissatisfied with the way their bodies look. Losing weight is for people who know that they weigh more than what is ideal for their health. *Asking your doctor or nurse* what weight is recommended for your height, activity level, size, and age will help you make wise choices.

. . . .

Can you talk a little bit about ANOREXIA?

Anorexia nervosa is a condition in which someone chooses to limit the amount of food they eat or increase the amount of exercise they do to lose weight *beyond what is healthy for their body*. Anorexia nervosa occurs when someone has the idea that their body is "fat" and that they need to lose an excessive amount of weight even if their body needs more weight to function well. People who experience anorexia nervosa require support and help from experts to understand how to keep their bodies at a healthy weight. It's important to *talk to a trusted adult* if you feel like you are overly concerned about losing weight or if you feel a friend is struggling with this problem.

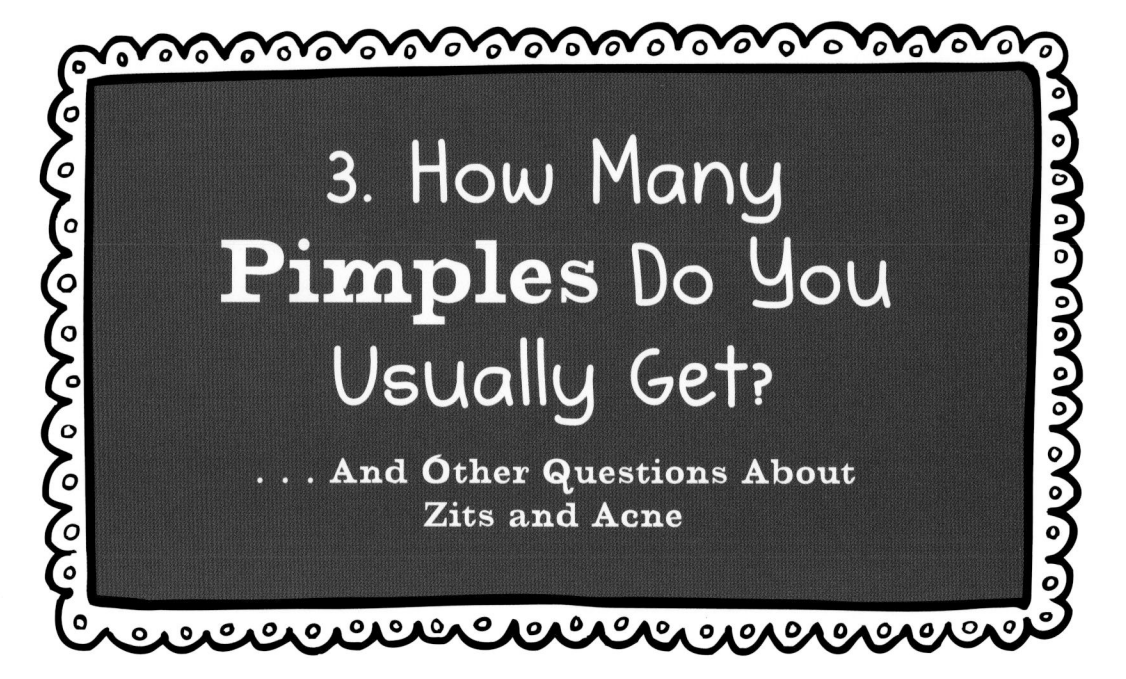

3. How Many Pimples Do You Usually Get?

. . . And Other Questions About Zits and Acne

I am NOT looking forward to having pimples . . . what do I do to handle them?

Keeping your skin clean every day by washing it with a mild soap or cleanser can reduce the amount of germs and bacteria on it. Washing your skin also creates less opportunity for them to be trapped and create a pimple. But it will not prevent all pimples. Sometimes no matter what we do, pimples show up.

For the occasional pimple that everyone gets, the ingredients found to be most effective in pimple management are *benzoyl peroxide* and *salicylic acid*. You can find pimple-treating products with benzoyl peroxide or salicylic acid in a regular grocery store or in your neighborhood pharmacy. There are additional solutions that can be very effective in helping your skin clear up as well. *Getting advice from a physician* is a great next step if you need more information. The good news is that as we get older, our skin gets less oily over time and most people experience pimples less frequently.

ZIT CREAM

HOW BIG do pimples get? (I hope not too big, it would be sort of embarrassing.)

Because pimples are uninvited interruptions to our otherwise dazzling good looks *and* appear on our faces, necks, chests, and backs, they can definitely be annoying and sometimes even embarrassing. The good news is that you can be certain that almost every single human being knows what a pain a pimple can be, either because they have had one or because they will soon get one. Teasing someone about a pimple is only funny when yours is bigger. Pimples and other skin-related challenges like blackheads can be different sizes. The good news is, no matter how big pimples get, they *typically only last a few days* and there are ways of treating them when they show up.

. . . .

When will your pimples STOP GROWING? I've heard it can take 10 years.

Our skin changes throughout our lives. You don't often see a two-year-old with a lot of pimples, and you don't often see a ninety-two-year-old with a lot of pimples. When our bodies are going through puberty, the new hormones change some of the glands in our skin, causing them to produce more oil, and that oil can sometimes clog a pore with dead skin cells and bacteria. That then creates a small infection—or pimple. However, it is not uncommon for people to have *occasional* pimples throughout their adult lives as bacteria can get trapped even in less oily skin.

. . . .

How many pimples do you usually get?

Contrary to popular thinking, how many pimples you get does *not* have much to do with eating chocolate or drinking soda. There are many factors that contribute to how many pimples people experience—including things you *can't* control like your

puberty hormones and the skin type you inherit from your birth parents; and things you *can* control like how you take care of your skin. You may find that there are *certain foods or stresses* you experience that make you more susceptible to a breakout, so you can certainly pay attention to those—and they may be the same or different than what causes pimples for your good friend.

4. Some People Have Noticed That I Have a **Bad Smell.** What Should I Do About It?

. . . And Other Questions About Body Odor and Sweat

Some people have noticed that I have a BAD SMELL. What should I do about it?

Our bodies can create a lot of **unpleasant** smells—from sweaty underarms to farts to bad breath to stinky feet! Sometimes we don't even notice that we have all these smells because *our noses get used to our own bodies.* Usually, if people are mentioning a "bad smell" now that you are in puberty, it probably means it's time to **pay attention** to keeping your body clean! If you are not interested in having a sweaty smell all day, then **showering** or rinsing off your body on a regular basis so that there is less sweat and fewer bacteria to combine with your sweat would help. Places where sweat accumulates need special attention: under your arms, between your legs, and on the bottoms of your feet. Sometimes people  wear **deodorant** or antiperspirants under their arms in addition to showering. Antiperspirants reduce the amount of sweat on the skin where you apply it—often under your arms. That way, the sweat and bacteria

don't mix. Deodorants "deodorize," and change the smell of the sweat that has been broken down by bacteria. Deodorants allow your body to sweat. You can buy deodorants for foot odor as well. Since sweating is a good thing, *I recommend a deodorant* if you are looking for something beyond a shower. Don't forget about brushing your teeth and keeping your hair clean too—it's part of the whole package!

. . . .

When you are about 9 you get sweat under your arms—at what age does it stop?

Your **whole body** has actually had the ability to sweat since you were born; it's *how your body naturally cools off* when you get too warm. You will continue to sweat your entire life. What you may have noticed is that when you are in puberty, your body actually sweats *more*—especially under your arms. Sweat, by itself, does not have any particular smell. Once you start puberty, though, **hormonal** changes alter the composition of your sweat; when the sweat comes in contact with the bacteria that live naturally on your skin, it creates a stronger **odor**. A sweaty two-year-old smells different than a sweaty twelve-year-old.

. . . .

One of my friends has a lot of BO— should I tell her or not?

People's **perception** of body odor differs *across cultures and circumstances*. Body odor may seem perfectly fine in the locker room after basketball practice, but it may not be as pleasant at your family dinner table. Some people live in cultures where a sweaty smell is seen as a natural part of a hard day's work, while people in other cultures find it annoying and think it should be avoided. Most likely your friend will start to perceive her **body odor** with time. If you choose to bring it up with your friend, *you might include your own*

experience so that your friend will be less embarrassed: "I have sure been smelling sweaty lately—but I have a new favorite deodorant that smells like lemon that really works! You might like it too."

. . . .

I have noticed that eating certain foods changes the way I smell—is that possible?

Yes! Certain **foods** change the way our bodies smell in several different ways. Eating asparagus makes our urine smell different. Strong-tasting foods like garlic change our breath and sweat, and their smells can stay on our skin longer than other foods. Some foods create gasses in our digestive systems that come out as farts. Some people are more sensitive to certain foods and how their bodies process it, *so food can have different effects on different people.*

5. Why Do You Need a Bra in the First Place?

. . . And Other Questions About Breasts and Bras

I am in the 5th grade. Should I be wearing a bra? Why do you need a bra in the first place?

Although many of your friends and family members might wear a bra—many women in the world don't have access to bras, don't feel they need a bra, and don't even own one! There are **zero rules** about when someone has to wear a bra—in fifth grade *or any age*. There are all sorts of reasons people might choose to wear a bra. One reason is that bras **support** breasts. When running on the soccer field or jumping rope, girls often find wearing a bra *more comfortable*. Sometimes people wear one because they like the way their clothes look or feel when they wear it. Sometimes girls wear a bra entirely because they think they are "supposed to" since all of their friends wear them, and they want to look the same as their friends. *Throughout your life* you might make different **choices** of when you wear a bra. What is important is that you think through *what seems right for you*.

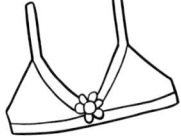 

My friends say I need a bra but I'm TOO EMBARRASSED to ask for one. What should I do?

Feeling embarrassed is a pretty **natural feeling**. It's not like you have had a lot of opportunities to ask for a bra before, and having breasts is also a new experience. No one needs to buy a bra because her friends say so. If you think it would be helpful to have a bra to support your breasts, or because it would be interesting, comfortable, or you are curious, sometimes asking a trusted adult is the most **challenging** part. This is probably because saying out loud that you would like to have a bra can feel like you are announcing to the world in a loud voice, **I have breasts**. Sometimes the easiest way to ask about something that is embarrassing is to *wait until you are alone with a trusted adult*—like a parent, aunt, grandparent, or teacher. Maybe when you are sitting together in a car or walking side-by-side, when you feel **ready**, you could say something like, "I was thinking it would be kind of interesting to look into getting a bra. Would you be able to help me with that?"

. . . .

How do I ask my mom for a padded bra because I really want one?

Women wear **padded bras** when they would like their breasts to appear bigger, or be a different shape, than they are naturally. When someone has had surgery on a breast or is wearing special clothes that need a certain fit, it can sometimes be helpful to have additional support or padding. You might want to **think through** what your reasons are *for wanting a padded bra*. Sometimes people think that a certain size or shape of breast is more beautiful or interesting, when beauty is never actually limited to a single body part.

Questions About Breasts and Bras 19

My friend told me if you eat a lot of corn, you grow breasts faster. Is this true?

There aren't any specific foods that make breasts grow faster, or bigger, or differently. How fast our bodies grow and how large or small our breasts are have a lot to do with our birth parents and the size of their bodies and breasts. It also has something to do with how we take care of our bodies—with enough food, sleep, and exercise. Every body is unique, and the size and pace of puberty cannot be determined by a single food. However, our bodies need to have enough of the right foods to grow well overall (see page 8 for more on healthy eating).

. . . .

HOW LONG does it take for breasts to grow?

Your breasts start as small bumps underneath your nipples. You may have noticed small bumps—or you may have noticed that when someone runs into you in the hall or gives you a big hug, your nipples feel tender, almost like they are bruised. The bumps and the tenderness are evidence that breast tissue is developing. It usually takes a couple of years for breasts to fully develop. However, even when breasts are finished growing, they continue to change their size and shape throughout your life. It may seem to you like breasts are supposed to look a certain way, but there are as many different shapes and sizes of breasts as there are women in the world.

. . . .

One of my breasts has been bigger than my other one for a while—IS THIS NORMAL?

Because you have two breasts side by side, you might think that they would grow together at the exact same time in the exact same way. But in fact, breasts grow independently from each other. It's not unusual for one breast to start

developing for a month or two before the other breast begins to grow. Even when they are finished growing, it would be completely typical for one breast to look **bigger** or be **different** in shape from the other breast.

. . . .

I have a cat that pushes down on my breasts, will it damage them?

Breasts are **resilient** to cats pushing down on them—also dogs, hamsters, and turtles! Sometimes when breasts are developing, they can feel **tender**—almost like a bruise—when they are touched or bumped or pushed down on by cats. That feeling *is just breast tissue growing* and tends to go away in a couple of years when breasts have finished growing.

. . . .

What are the STRETCH MARKS for on your breasts?

Stretch marks happen on places of your body where your skin has experienced **rapid growth** or weight gain. The "marks" are where layers of skin can have different colors from the skin **stretching**. Not everyone gets stretch marks, and some people get them on places other than their breasts. Stretch marks will sometimes go away or become less visible over time. They do not change how breasts or other body parts work. *Boys get stretch marks too*—and so do adult men and women.

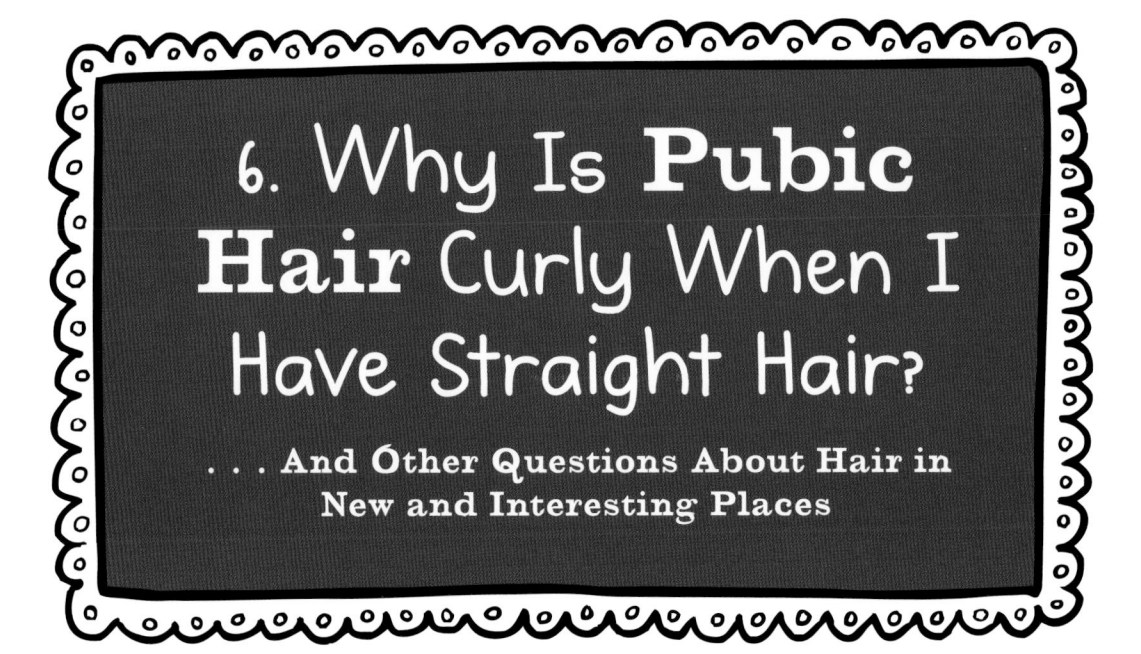

6. Why Is **Pubic Hair** Curly When I Have Straight Hair?

. . . And Other Questions About Hair in New and Interesting Places

When is the average age of someone who shaves their legs?

Across cultures and throughout history, there have been different ideas and practices for women removing **body hair**. There are all sorts of reasons someone might choose to remove body hair—beauty, sports, religion, tradition, comfort, because their friends and family do. And there are all sorts of reasons that women would *never* remove body hair—beauty, sports, religion, tradition, comfort, and because their friends and family *don't*. Millions of women around the world leave their body hair to **grow** and don't cut it, shave it, or wax it, and millions of women regularly remove their body hair. I bet if we asked all the women from around the world at what age they began shaving their legs, there would be so many women that don't shave their legs that the *average age* would be **never**. You might find that when you ask *your* friends or women in *your* family, you get a different answer because in the place you live women choose to remove body hair. In the end, it's **your choice**.

My grandma told me that once I shave my legs, I need to shave my legs the REST OF MY LIFE. Is that true?

Sometimes people think if you **shave** your legs, the hair on your legs will change forever—that you will have more hair and that it will be darker and more coarse. When you use a **razor** to shave hair and it begins to grow back, the hair sometimes seems darker and feels **prickly**. But actually shaving or waxing your hair does not change the color or the hair itself—it just appears that way when it first grows back. This is because shaving cuts each individual hair shaft off at a sharp edge so that when it first grows back, *it's not as soft*. But if you were to let the hair grow out again, with time the hair would eventually appear like it did before you started shaving. Hair darkens on most people as they get older *but not because they shave* their hair.

. . . .

When you have ARMPIT HAIR is it OK if you cut it with scissors or is it better to shave it?

Cutting your underarm hair with scissors would definitely be **tricky!** There are a number of **safer ways** to remove hair from under your arms or other places if you decide that is something that is important to you. Most women who are interested in removing their hair use a **razor** on wet, lubricated skin (using lotion or soap as a lubricant helps the razor glide on the skin more easily and reduces the possibility of irritation). Other women choose to **wax** their hair. This involves applying a warm liquid wax and then pulling the wax off quickly—much like removing a bandage. (I recommend having an expert help you with this if you think it sounds interesting to try.) *Removing body hair* can sometimes create irritated skin or cause a hair to grow back at an angle into the skin (this is called an "ingrown hair"), creating an infection that is easily treatable but sometimes irritating.

How much hair do you get in your armpits if you don't shave? (In inches.)

The *thickness, color, and length* of your hair usually follows patterns established by family genetics—the messages we receive about our bodies from our **birth parents** and their parents. However, most underarm hair does not get longer than *a few inches* even if you don't cut or shave it.

I am questioning the hair. Does it hurt when it grows?

Hair **doesn't hurt** as it grows. *Your hair doesn't have any nerves* (the threads connected to our brains that communicate pain), which is why it doesn't hurt when you cut hair either.

. . . .

Can you wake up one day and have a lot of pubic hair?

It is possible that one day you'll be in the shower and you'll become **suddenly aware** that you have pubic hair that you never noticed before. Sometimes that is because *we are not always paying attention*—especially during everyday events like taking a shower—to all the different parts of our bodies. Pubic hair can be difficult to spot when it first starts growing, since it starts slowly and its color can blend into the hair that's already on your body. Pubic hair often becomes coarser in texture and darker as we get older.

. . . .

What is the point of pubic hair?

What an intriguing question! It hardly seems like we need **pubic hair** to stay warm or to make us more interesting, since most of the time it is hidden from view. Most likely, pubic hair is left over from *millions of years ago*, before people had clothes and they needed more hair **covering** them to keep them warm. It's a bit of a mystery!

Why is pubic hair curly when I have straight hair?

Wild, isn't it? Because pubic hair and underarm hair are a part of our puberty experience, they are the result of our **hormones** changing. Hormones also seem to sometimes affect hair follicles—the areas in the skin where hair grows. The hair **follicles** in your underarms and between your legs are actually a different shape than the hair follicles on your head where straight hair grows. These differently shaped follicles can create *curly hairs*.

. . . .

What should I do about pubic hair if I swim?

If you are asking what to do if you think others can see your pubic hair when you wear your **swimsuit** and that doesn't feel comfortable to you, there are ways to remove hair through *shaving*, *waxing* or using *hair-removing lotions*. It's important to remember that pubic hair is a **human experience**—one that happens to all people around the world. Remembering that someone who notices your pubic hair would be seeing something that also happens to them might help you feel less self-conscious.

. . . .

Does puberty make all of your hair curly—even on your head?

It is quite **common** that our hormones will **change** the curliness of all of our hair—*not just pubic and underarm hair*. Sometimes people in puberty will go from straight or wavy hair on their heads to very curly hair, or from curly hair to straight or wavy hair!

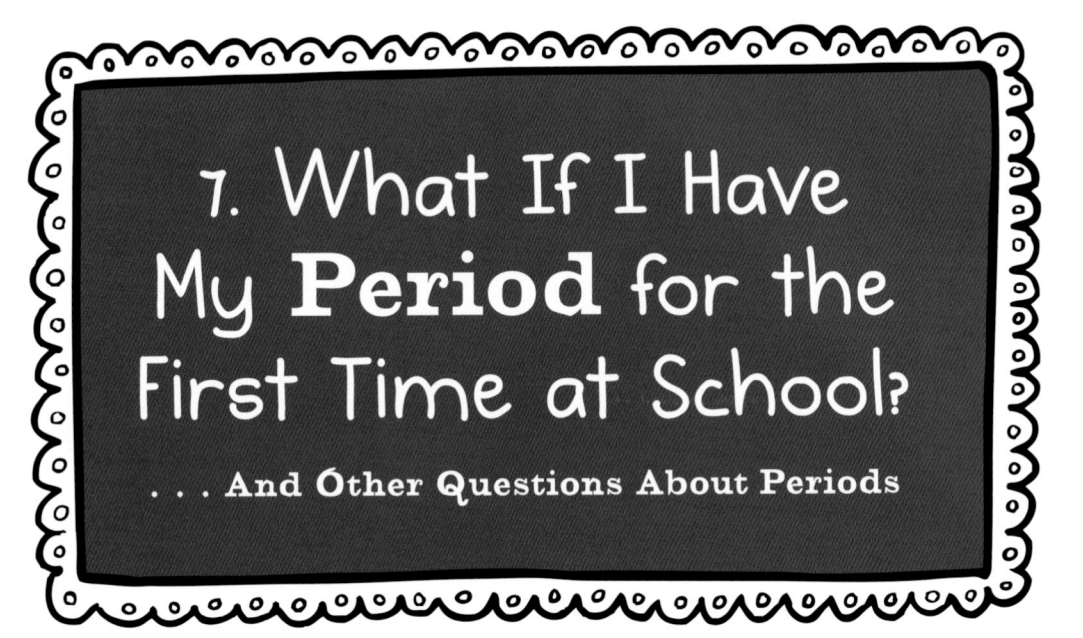

7. What If I Have My **Period** for the First Time at School?

. . . And Other Questions About Periods

So, what is a PERIOD exactly?

The last *new* thing that happens to a girl's body during puberty is the beginning of her period. As your body grows and develops on the outside, it grows and changes on the inside as well. (To understand these internal changes, it helps to have a picture of all the body parts involved—turn to page 31 and take a look.) You have a uterus that is found inside your body just below your belly button and above your pubic bone. Your uterus is about the size of your fist—so a baby girl's uterus is much smaller than an adult's uterus. The uterus is where the baby grows while a woman is pregnant—so just picture how big it can get! Attached to the uterus are two fallopian tubes and connected to those tubes are ovaries. (An ovary in an adult woman is about the size of a large olive.) Inside your two ovaries are *millions of eggs*—microscopic cells that have been there since you were born. Now that you are in puberty, hormones signal an egg to be released one at a time from an ovary. The egg travels into the fallopian tube and then into the uterus. While the tiny egg is traveling, a cup or so of fluid is collecting in the uterus getting ready for the egg's arrival. Since this egg is traveling alone

and not meeting up with a sperm (more on sperm and eggs meeting up in Chapter 13), the egg and the fluid leave from your body through your vagina. The fluid, which contains a tablespoon or two of blood, and the tiny egg that leave your body are called a period. The entire process from the egg being released to its leaving your body is called menstruation or *menstrual cycle*.

Why is it called MENstruation? Why MEN?

That's an excellent question! The official word for a period is menstruation—but many people call the experience a period. And since *men* do not have menstruation, it seems an especially odd choice. I really think a better name would be *women*struation, don't you? The word menstruation actually comes from the word menses, which means "month"—and women typically have periods monthly.

Can you predict when your first period will be?

Although it's *impossible to predict the exact day* your first period will appear, your body provides some clues that can tell you the general time that your body is preparing for having your first period. First, your body needs to be close to its adult size to begin having a period. Sometimes the leanest girls—either tall or short—are the last to start their periods because their bodies haven't gotten close enough to an adult weight yet. Second, most girls have pubic hair before they have their first period. Third, many girls notice a small amount of fluid—a white sticky substance in their underwear—that shows up occasionally and may occur months before their period. This is nothing to worry about—it's just fluid from your vagina that shows you that your body is getting ready for a period. You will have that same fluid before your first period and before every period throughout your period life. And finally, the average age for a girl in the United States to start her period is about twelve years old. "Average" means that there are girls who are starting their periods at age nine or earlier and girls who are starting at age fourteen or later.

Does your period last forever?

Periods last for a period of your life. You start your period during puberty and you stop having periods when you're about fifty years old.

. . . .

Did you say that your period lasts 4-7 days or 47 days?

The time of fluid leaving our bodies *typically lasts 4 to 7 days and nights*; although some women have periods that last a few days more or less.

. . . .

I'm only 11 and I have my period. I'm the only one in my class, and I'm really embarrassed. WHAT SHOULD I DO?

Eleven is a very typical age to start having a period. And, unless you have asked all the girls in your class, you may not be the only one who has started since you really can't tell from looking at someone whether she has had her period or not. Being self-conscious and shy about having your period is not unusual—*it's a new experience*, and you need to get used to everything involved with it. I am confident that even if you are the first, it won't be long until others are also having periods. Sometimes it's helpful to recognize that being first is like being a pioneer—soon, others might be looking to you for ideas since you will be the one *with the most experience!*

. . . .

What do you do if you've been waiting, waiting, waiting, and YOUR PERIOD doesn't happen?

The entire experience of puberty takes several years—periods start a couple of years after you notice your breasts beginning to develop. When all of your friends

have gone through puberty faster than you have, it can feel like it takes forever. Sometimes it can be especially challenging because everyone is talking about something you haven't experienced yet. Remember, your experience will be *uniquely your own*. However, if you feel like you are still waiting for some of the signs that your period will start and you are fourteen years old or older, it is helpful to talk to a doctor or nurse to check in and get more information.

. . . .

What is it like when you first get your period? What is your first feeling?

When a period starts—whether it is your first period or your two-hundredth period—you may first notice a small amount of warm wetness between your legs. Sometimes it is difficult to tell that your period has started until you go to the bathroom to check. You will be able to tell because period fluid is reddish in color, from the small amount of blood present, so you will see it on your underwear and possibly on your pants or other clothing. Your first period may look very dark red or brown in color.

. . . .

Do you start out with pads, tampons, or what?

Because your period is red, it will show up on your clothes if you don't protect them. Today, there are several options to take care of this. Two popular choices are pads and tampons. Many girls like to start with pads because they are the simplest to figure out. Keep reading!

. . . .

Why do women wear the pads on their vagina?

Made of cottony material, pads are worn *inside your underwear* on the *outside of your body* during a period. There are all different sizes of pads—long, short, thin,

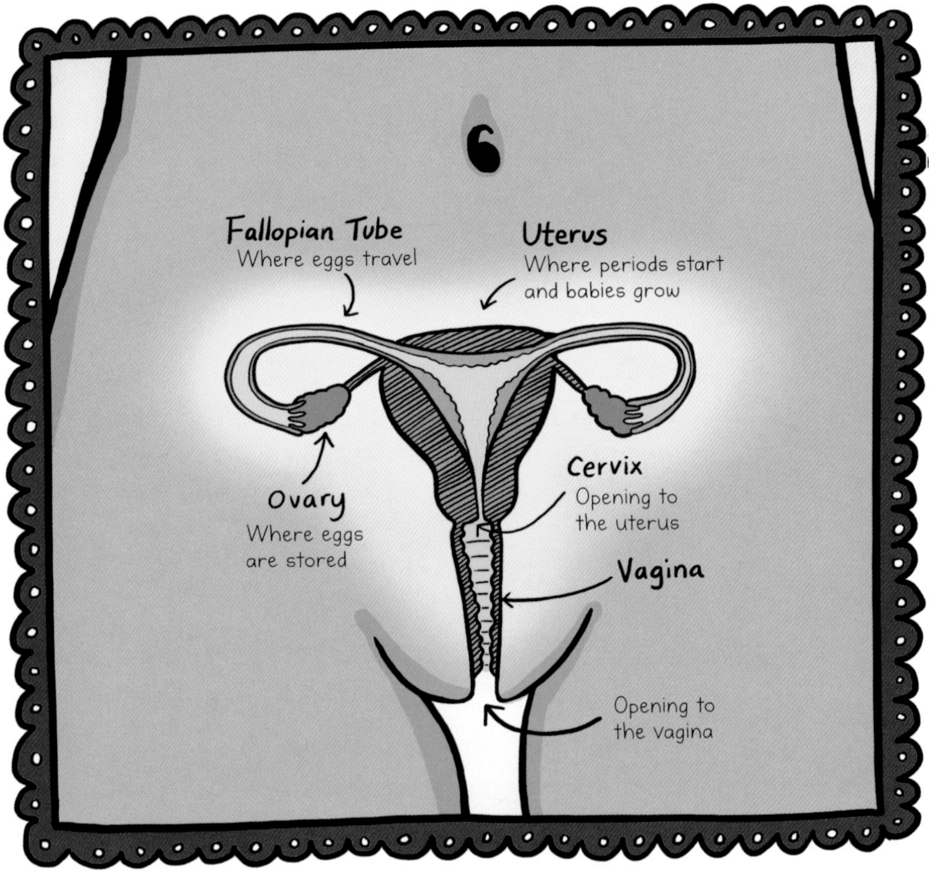

Fallopian Tube
Where eggs travel

Uterus
Where periods start and babies grow

Ovary
Where eggs are stored

Cervix
Opening to the uterus

Vagina

Opening to the vagina

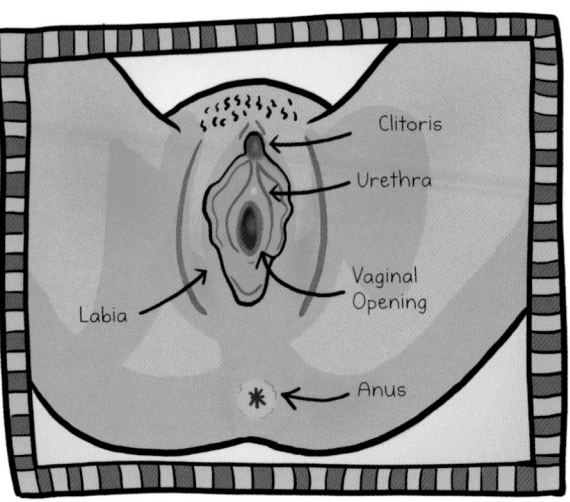

Clitoris

Urethra

Labia

Vaginal Opening

Anus

or thick. *Some even have wings!* They catch the period fluid by absorbing it after it leaves your vagina. You wear the pad during the days and nights you have a period. You change your pad throughout the day as needed. On a typical period day, you might change a pad five to ten times. Most pads attach to your underwear with an adhesive strip, so it is very easy to put on and take off and stays in place even on a busy and active day. Some pads are disposable, so when you are ready to change it, you throw it in the garbage wrapped in a small amount of toilet paper; some pads are made from cloth so that they are reusable once you have washed and dried them. *Pads have changed a lot throughout history*—ask someone a generation or two older than you what pads were like when they were your age and you'll be surprised at the answer!

· ·

Can I wear a tampon?

Like pads, tampons absorb the fluid of your period—but instead of being on the outside of your body like a pad, a tampon goes inside your vagina to *absorb the fluid before it leaves your body*. Putting in a tampon takes motivation and a bit of practice, but any girl can try it. Some girls wait to try a tampon until they are older or have had some time getting used to the other logistics of a period. Some women never wear a tampon. It's possible to try a tampon the very *first* minute of your very *first* period.

Tampons come in *several sizes*, and not all tampons have applicators. If you are thinking about trying a tampon, it's helpful to start with the smallest-sized tampon and one with an applicator. Applicators are made of cardboard or plastic— some girls find the plastic applicators to be an easier place to start. Spending some time looking at a tampon before you try to put it in is a good idea—open up the package and take one apart to see how it all works together.

How do you stick a tampon in your vagina?

When you are ready to try a tampon, first use the toilet if you need to so that you can relax all the muscles you typically use to hold back urine. While continuing to sit on the toilet, open up any packaging or paper surrounding the tampon applicator. You will see ridges in the center where you put your thumb and middle finger. Your index finger rests on the end where the string comes out. Using your other hand, open the lips of your labia and place the tip of the applicator (the opposite end from the string) up against your vagina. (A picture of how this all looks helps a lot! Check out page 31 to see these body parts up close.) The key idea here is to insert the tip of the applicator at an angle that points toward your backbone. Your vagina is actually tilted at an angle to your back. After inserting the applicator tip, you can begin to push the plunger on the applicator with your index finger while holding the ridges in the center of the applicator so that the tampon will *slide into your vagina.* When your index finger has pushed the end up to the ridges, you can pull the applicator out, leaving the tampon in—with the string outside of your body. *You did it!* The string will be helpful in removing the tampon. Keep reading!

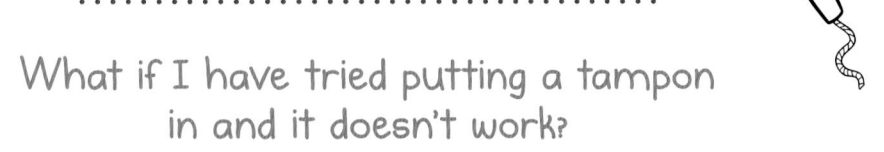

What if I have tried putting a tampon in and it doesn't work?

Don't worry if it doesn't feel *like a smooth process* the first time, or even if it doesn't work out—it often takes a few times to get used to the logistics. A girl also has a thin membrane covering the opening of her vagina called a hymen that can sometimes make trying a tampon more challenging. Your hymen can be stretched or torn from day-to-day activities like riding a bike or having period fluid come out. But if your hymen has not been stretched or broken, the tampon might meet resistance. If you don't have success on the first attempt, you can always try later. In the meantime, pads are a great alternative. It can be helpful if you have an adult or older girl to talk you through the logistics. There are also instructions in the boxes of tampons for additional information and help.

What if I accidentally put the tampon in the wrong hole? Or in too far?

It can be helpful to be familiar with how your body looks between your legs so that you can find your vagina more easily. Using a mirror and spending a minute finding your vagina will *make things a bit easier*. As a girl, you have three openings between your legs: your urethra, where urine (pee) leaves your bladder; your vagina, which leads to your uterus; and your anus, where undigested waste (poop) leaves your body. You do not need to worry about accidentally putting a tampon in your urethra—*it is far too small*. And if you accidentally put a tampon in your anus, you would recognize you were in the wrong spot by how it feels.

It is impossible to put a tampon in too far—you do not need to worry about it getting lost and floating around in your body so that it comes out of your ear in social studies class! Your cervix will keep a tampon from going any further than where it belongs. (Check out the picture on page 31 to see all these body parts!)

. . . .

Tampons kind of scare me. Pushing something inside my body—could I hurt myself?

One of the easiest mistakes to make as you are practicing and learning how to put a tampon in is to not get it in far enough. The muscles surrounding our vagina are strong, so when a tampon is inserted only part of the way, the muscles surrounding the tampon will tighten around it and make standing up without pain difficult. If this happens, the thing to do is to remove the tampon and start over with a new one.

The good news about wearing a tampon is that when it is in correctly, *you cannot feel it*. The bad news about wearing a tampon correctly is that you cannot feel it. That means it's *possible* to forget you have a tampon in! When women wear the same tampon for too long because they forgot about it, bacteria can grow and make them sick—called *toxic shock*. Wearing a tampon requires remembering to take it out and replace it with another tampon

or a pad during the four to seven days and nights of your period. You will know it is time to change your tampon when you can sense that it is no longer being helpful in absorbing fluid.

A great idea is to change your tampon every time you go to the bathroom, or *about every four hours*. Remove your tampon by pulling on the string gently, remembering to keep those muscles relaxed—*it will slide right out*. Wrap up the tampon in toilet paper and throw it in the garbage. Some women only wear a tampon when they would find it more helpful than a pad—like when they are swimming or playing sports—and they wear a pad other times of the day and night.

. . . .

What if I have my period for the first time at school? And what if I have my period during a piano lesson in the middle of a really long Bach piece?!

There are two *guaranteed* things about a period: first, the exact moment it starts will be a surprise; and second, there are all sorts of people who can help problem-solve with you. Being caught off guard by your period requires creativity and ingenuity—and creative and ingenious is just what you are!

Whether you are in math class or at a piano lesson, when your period starts, it can be very distracting, but it is *not an emergency*. Asking the teacher to be excused for a minute to go to the restroom is a good start. If your period has started and you are worried that people will notice period fluid on the back of your clothes while you're walking to the bathroom, you can wrap something like a sweatshirt around your waist, or pull your shirt out to cover your pants or skirt. If you forgot your sweatshirt, you can hold something like a book or a backpack behind you as you exit. If you are somewhere where you don't have a tampon or a pad, you can make a temporary pad out of toilet paper. Generally, *unless you draw attention to your challenging moment*, other people are not looking for periods on people.

The thing I am most worried about is will people know just by looking at me that I had my period?

If your clothes are **protected** with a pad, a tampon, or even a "pad" you have made from toilet paper, no one will be able to tell from looking at you. Taking a **shower** every day when you are having a period keeps your body clean and removes any of the period fluid that can create an odor over time. By *taking care of yourself and your body* during your period, you'll be sure that no one will be able to tell unless you bring it up. Wild as it is to think about, you are probably around women all the time who are having their periods—in the grocery store, at school, coaching volleyball, or on the chess team. They're **all around** you, and you have never noticed they were having a period.

No one is required to know if you are having your period, but if it feels helpful to you to let someone know in order to get support or help, *speak up!* Typically there is someone in a school office responsible for the students' health—like a nurse—who has pads and other supplies and is prepared to help you. Also, in the office there is often backup clothing and a chance to call someone if you need to. Camp counselors, and piano teachers, soccer coaches, and chess club advisors will *all* be understanding if you need to bring them in to help you navigate the *logistics of a period.*

. . . .

Is it uncomfortable to have a period at night?

It is no more uncomfortable to have a period at night than during the day. You don't need to worry about setting an alarm clock to wake up every four hours to change a tampon at night—just wear a **pad** instead.

What do you do if you get your period while you're swimming? Freaked out!

Swimming while having a period requires some thought and planning, so let's talk it through so that you won't need to freak out in the moment. There are a couple of *challenges to consider*. First, if you are wearing just a swimsuit and your period starts, it will be more apparent than if you were wearing a pair of jeans or shorts, because the red fluid of your period won't have a second layer of clothing to keep it contained. Second, if you wear a pad to protect your swimsuit, it is easy to see the pad because it is on the outside of your body. And third, a pad can't distinguish between period fluid and pool water, so a pad won't really absorb period fluid if you are swimming with it on.

What can you do? Remember, period fluid only comes out a small amount at a time. So if you have your period and you want to jump in the ocean to cool off on a hot day or swim in a relay at the swim meet, taking off your pad and being in the water for a short amount of time is not a problem. You will want to put a pad back on, and maybe a pair of shorts or a swim cover-up, if you sit on the beach to hang out or build a sand castle. Many times girls who are swimmers or who spend a lot of time at the beach find that wearing a tampon works best since tampons *absorb the fluid inside of your vagina*.

. . . .

The first time a period happens, do most girls feel uncomfortable or scared?

There are girls all over the world who have never had an opportunity to talk to someone about periods before their own show up. I can imagine that seeing reddish fluid in my underwear would be frightening if I had not had anyone tell me that it might happen. I can also imagine that there are girls who feel nervous about getting their periods *even when* they know everything there is to know about periods. But

there are also girls who look forward to getting their periods because they want to be part of something important. Periods show us that our bodies are becoming adult and that they are developing in a healthy way.

. . . .

How can I tell my mom if I started my period?

Talking to people (even your mom) about your period can seem awkward or scary because it is something brand new and seems kind of unusual. Sometimes we're not even sure how we feel about it ourselves. *Remember*, some moms have never had practice talking about periods either—perhaps they never talked to their mothers when they started their own periods. That means they feel just as shy or uncertain about the conversation as you do. Your mom might have some helpful ideas on how you can manage your period throughout your day and she wants this to go well for you. *Finding a moment* when you are alone with your mom—maybe while you're walking the dog or riding in the car can be a good time to start a conversation: "I just wanted you to know that my period started today."

. . . .

DOES IT HURT? Why do some girls feel icky when they have their period? I hear some girls throw up!

If you put one hundred women in a room and ask them if anything about having their periods "hurts" or "feels icky," some of the women would say "yes, absolutely," some would say "not really," and the rest would say "sometimes yes and sometimes no." Not everyone who has a period feels "icky" or throws up or has a painful experience. However, *some do*. It is also common for a woman to experience discomfort during some periods and not during others.

Some of the experiences that "feel icky" might include having a headache, lower backache, upset stomach, sensitive breasts, or cramps in your uterus. Often these feelings are more apparent in the first couple days of a period and improve toward the end of a period. Taking care of your body and treating the pain or discomfort

is important. *Staying active, exercising, and stretching* are often the most helpful ways to relieve some of these feelings. Some people find that putting something warm on their lower backs or lower bellies helps.

It is a *good idea to ask for help* if you find that how you feel during your periods is keeping you from the activities that you usually enjoy. A doctor or nurse practitioner often has helpful solutions for your specific needs.

Your grandmothers and great grandmothers were cautioned not to play sports or dance when they had their periods. They were often also told not to go to the dentist or have their hair curled, or even washed, while menstruating. Today we know it is important for girls to stay active, eat and drink healthy foods, and get adequate sleep during their periods—the *best ways* to care for their bodies.

. . . .

What do you think might happen when a CAVE WOMAN had their period?

Because there isn't much information about the daily lives of cave women, we can only imagine some of the ways they managed their periods. One way might have been that they wore *animal skins* or used *plants* to help absorb their periods. It might even have been that nobody noticed or cared. Or they might have had a special place that women gathered during their periods where they would stay together while they were menstruating.

It's interesting to think of women across history and the challenges they may have faced. I often think about women today, and throughout time, who have walked long distances over many days or months while menstruating—like crossing the Oregon Trail as pioneers, or crossing a desert in a caravan. Those women have *managed their periods* without being able to run to the grocery store to get supplies. There are girls who live in places even today who do not have access to pads and tampons. They would have different choices to make about managing their periods than you do.

Is it true you STOP GROWING when you start your period?

The very last *new* thing that happens to you during puberty is starting your period. But puberty doesn't officially end until you stop growing. Typically, when a girl's period starts she still has some growing to do—maybe a couple of inches, but probably not ten! By the time your period starts, the *majority of your growing* has occurred.

. . . .

Why is chocolate such a big asset to having a period, as a helpful thing?

Sometimes you hear women talk about how a few days before their periods they crave certain foods. Researchers have tried to find out if women want certain foods for a reason, but they still have more questions than answers. What we *do* know is that how we take care of our bodies during our periods is important—we need to continue to eat a diet that includes calcium, fruits, vegetables, grains, iron, and protein. Sadly, it is not recommended for girls to *only* eat chocolate!

. . . .

How do you make your period MORE FUN?

Our diverse culture doesn't have a shared tradition to celebrate when girls start their periods or finish puberty, and many girls I talk to can't imagine drawing attention to the whole thing. However, in *some cultures around the world*, a girl's first period, or finishing puberty, is celebrated—it's a time of honor as a girl's body becomes like an adult woman's. In Japan, some girls eat a special meal of red rice and almonds when they get their first period. In South Africa, girls might receive beautiful red beaded bracelets to mark the occasion. In parts of India, girls are honored at parties that include traditional foods, saris, and jewelry. In parts of Eastern

Asia, girls who have started their periods live in white huts, wear white clothes, and eat white foods for a whole year. In Jewish culture, some girls study to have bat mitzvahs, where they assume the new responsibilities of adulthood in their communities. My neighbor and her mother chose to mark the occasion of her first period with a special dinner together in a favorite restaurant. Perhaps thinking of a way to celebrate with a parent or friend would be a way to honor this transition—sounds like a lot of fun!

. . . .

If you have a period at a certain time does it change you?

Having a period will change some of the day-to-day things you do during the four to seven days of menstruation. However, it does not have to change the person that you are *or the person that you are becoming*. Remember, there are women who have competed in the Olympics, and won gold medals while having a period. There are women who have written beautiful poetry and prize-winning literature while having a period. There are women who have campaigned for social justice, lived in jungles and deserts, fought in combat, and traveled in space shuttles, all while having a period. Although it can feel a bit overwhelming at the beginning, and even a bit scary as you hear about it for the first time, women all over the world and throughout history have managed periods while they do other important work.

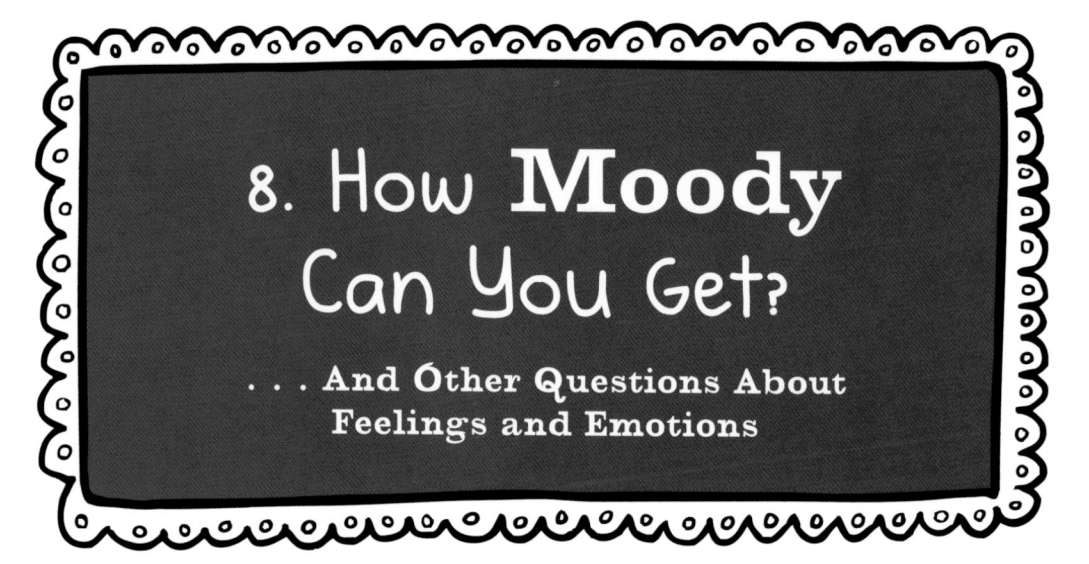

8. How **Moody** Can You Get?

. . . And Other Questions About Feelings and Emotions

How should I deal with my feelings if I feel a zillion things at once and don't know who to tell or what?

When you feel **overwhelmed** by your emotions, a good place to start is to give your feelings a name. If you find your face red, your stomach upset, and your voice loud, perhaps you could label your emotion "mad," "frustrated," or "discouraged." When you feel quiet, kind of shaky, and unable to talk without tears in your eyes, perhaps you can call that emotion "sad," "disappointed," or "embarrassed." *By labeling our emotions and feelings*, we help our brains define them, and when we define our **emotions**, we get better at finding specific **solutions** to manage them. Sometimes *writing in a journal* can be helpful since it gives you a place to describe how your body feels and the situation that made it feel that way. By writing these things down, you may be able to have a better understanding of why you feel the way you do, and when you have a better understanding, solutions may become clearer. Many people find that talking with a **trusted** person is helpful. For some kids that might be a parent, family member, or older sibling. For others, that might be a counselor or other expert.

How moody can you get?

Sometimes people say teenagers are "moody"—or have a lot of moods—because it's easy to tell what a teenager is feeling by what they are doing or saying. Teenagers express their moods more often than adults. The emotion center of a teenager's brain is very active. This is partially because the hormones responsible for puberty add to the excitement our brains feel when we have emotions—almost like *turning up the volume on a radio*. But it also has to do with the way our brains develop. Between the time of puberty and our early twenties, our brains build connections to parts of our brain where we learn how to manage our feelings when we make decisions. While our bodies are under construction, our brains are under construction too!

. . . .

Do you still have mood swings when you are older?

Yes! All people have moods that change throughout a day or an event. Since adult brains have had more experiences and more time to be wired, many times adults will not act on as many feelings as someone younger will. So, even though older adults have many emotions throughout a day, sometimes we don't see them in how the adults look and act.

. . . .

Do mood swings always make you GRUMPY? Thanks!

A mood swing is when your mood quickly changes from one mood to another. It could mean you are happy one minute and then sad the next. It could mean that you are grumpy in the morning at breakfast, but then you are laughing loudly at lunch. Sometimes people talk about mood swings only when someone's mood is negative, but mood swings happen any time our moods change. Having different

feelings throughout the day is a natural part of the way our brains work. Learning how to manage and communicate our emotions in healthy ways is one of the most important parts of growing up.

. . . .

Why do I CRY when I do not know why?

Crying has been a helpful part of your communication your whole life. When you were little and didn't have the language skills you have now, it was one of the only ways you could communicate fear, hunger, or a wet diaper. *Even as we get older*, sometimes crying offers a physical relief that helps manage or communicate our feelings. Working on finding words to *express your feelings* sometimes helps replace crying in situations where crying is not as helpful. But sometimes when we are very emotional, we use the response that has been the most useful in the past.

. . . .

I have been getting mad really easily at home and with my friends. Does that have anything to do with puberty?

Getting mad is a normal part of the human experience—it can communicate disappointment, discouragement, embarrassment, or something else. Sometimes if your emotional response is *big*, it's helpful to remember to take a break for a moment and give your body a chance to get calm. Taking deep breaths, listening to some music, or getting some exercise are all helpful options. It is almost impossible to come up with good solutions to challenges when we feel super angry. However, it's also important to *pay attention* to situations where you find yourself mad because it might give you insight into something that is important to you.

Why do I feel SO self-conscious?!

Going through puberty is like having your **body** and your **brain** under construction. There are many changes to get used to, like learning how to take care of your skin and managing your period, more sweat, and new hair. *That is a lot of work!* In addition, you are experiencing new emotions and situations that you need to work through, and that takes a lot of thought as well. Most girls and guys in puberty feel like they are the center of attention and they worry that *everyone* in the room is noticing their pimple or that they have BO or that they are embarrassed. The good news for you is that when everyone is only thinking about **themselves**, perhaps they will be so busy worrying that *you* are going to notice *their* pimple that they might not see yours!

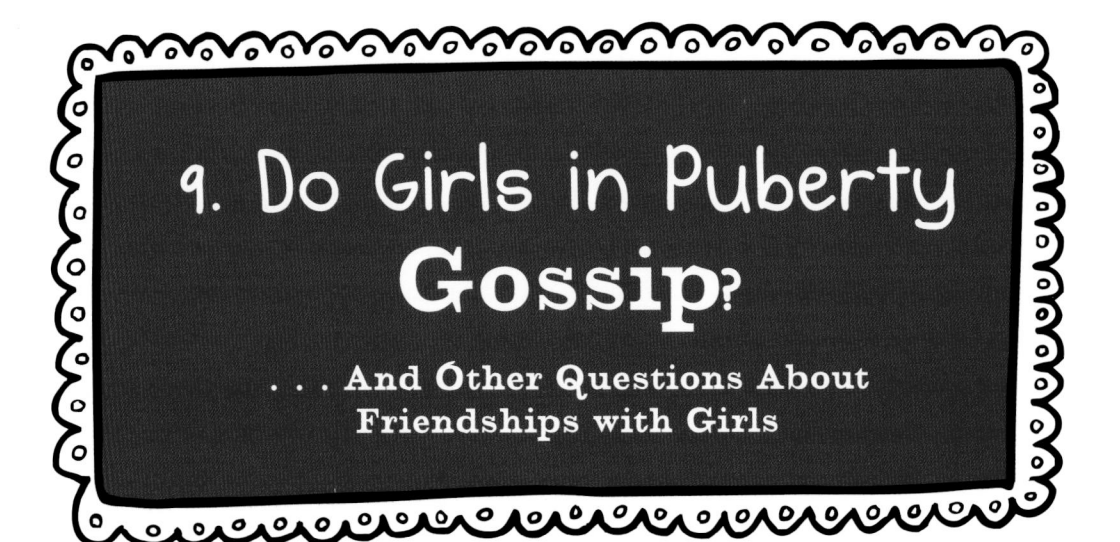

9. Do Girls in Puberty Gossip?

...And Other Questions About Friendships with Girls

What if a person you don't like is BEING TEASED, and you don't really want to stand up for them but you don't like seeing people get teased? Should you tell a grown-up, or do something else?

I haven't met a single person who hasn't experienced either being teased or watching someone else get teased. People often tease others when they feel afraid of something themselves. For instance, if a girl teases someone, she is trying to point out someone else's problem so that others don't point out her own concern. *We know two facts about teasing.* The first is that no one really looks forward to being teased, especially when it is unkind. The second thing we know is that if you hear someone being teased and you simply speak up or help redirect the subject, instead of adding to the laughter or the teasing, often the teasing will stop. That's because if the teaser doesn't get a response, then they don't have an audience for their "joke." Talking to a grown-up can sometimes be helpful if you need someone to talk your ideas through with. Sometimes it can be a grown-up who *does* the teasing and they don't understand that their words are hurtful. Adults occasionally use teasing and sarcasm to try to be funny. In that case, it might be helpful to talk to another trusted adult that can help you *communicate your feelings*.

Do girls in puberty gossip?

Yes, sometimes they do. Gossiping means sharing information about someone with others when the person you are talking about is not there. Gossiping often includes sharing stories that are not your business to talk about—and sometimes may not even be true. Gossiping can be tempting because it points out another person's problem instead of yours. You can feel like you're part of the group when you join in on the gossip, but the problem is that the group is defined by *gossiping* instead of by something more meaningful. What makes gossiping unhealthy is that the person you are talking about does not have the opportunity to share his or her own version of the story. *Sadly, there is no age limit to gossiping*, and both genders do it—girls, boys, and adults all gossip. Somehow talking about other people negatively can make us feel more important, but it *doesn't help us be a good friend*.

. . . .

If two girls are always whispering and acting like you're interrupting their private joke, what should you do? HOW DOES ONE COPE?

Whispering is a lot like gossiping because you are sharing information without letting others in on the conversation. It is a way for people to feel like they're important because they have *something to say*. Healthy conversations among friends include laughter, debate, sharing your feelings, and honesty. You may need to *take a break* from these friends who whisper until they *choose a different way* to bring others into their conversation. I am certain you are not alone in your challenges with these two girls—I can imagine you would find others who would be interested in joining you in another activity.

Why would someone want to be popular by being mean?

When people are mean, sometimes it's because they are trying to feel important or more powerful by making other people feel bad. Sometimes they do it because deep down, they feel afraid or uncertain, so they *cover up their feelings* by acting big and powerful. The definition of being popular is when someone is well liked by many people. Sometimes people mix up being powerful with being popular, because powerful people *demand a lot of attention,* and people give it to them because they are afraid or worried about what will happen if they don't. It is rare that people are truly popular *and* mean—most likely people who are mean are powerful, but they are not actually popular. Truly popular people are the ones who are admired by others because they help them feel important and included.

· ·

What if you are in a fight with a friend and she thinks she's being nice and you are being mean, but you think the opposite?

Being a friend can be hard work. It can means doing something that isn't your first choice but is what your friend wants to do. It can mean asking your friend to forgive you, or sticking up for her when it isn't easy to do. It is inevitable that there are also times when friends do not get along. In this case, maybe you need to find out what you *do* agree on in this argument to find some common ground.

· ·

Can you tell us about peer PRESSURE?

Peer pressure is when you believe your friends or other kids want you to do something that you *otherwise would not choose to do.* Sometimes you hear them say their ideas out loud ("Come on! Don't be a chicken, just jump!") and sometimes they don't say anything out loud but you believe they want you to do something

("They are going to think I am a chicken if I don't jump."). What is important is that you make your own **decisions** in partnership with your family's support and input. It's hard when you feel like you are the *only one* not participating and that you will lose the friendship of others if you choose not to join in what they are doing. Sometimes you will find that if you choose something other than what the group is suggesting, others will be relieved and join you.

. . . .

Will girls in grade school who are not very kind be kind after they go through puberty?

During puberty, you are also learning about how to have healthy **friendships**. For some people, being kind is **hard work**—maybe because they haven't had much practice, or there aren't many people who are kind to them, or they feel more powerful when they are mean. There is no guarantee that when a girl is finished with puberty she will be more kind, though *hopefully over time* she will grow in her ability to be a better friend.

10. Do Boys Have Crushes on Us or Is It Just a Rumor?

. . . And Other Questions About Crushes, Dating, and Attractions

My best friend is a boy, and so far no one has teased us, but we're starting middle school next year and I've heard that sometimes people tease you if your best friend is a boy. What do I do?

Having a good friend is a wonderful thing. But being teased is not easy to manage, no matter what the circumstance. Since we can't really control what others say or do, it's helpful to have some ideas of what *you* might do if that happens. There are usually a couple of responses that are pretty effective. First, you can **ignore** the comment. Sometimes when you don't give someone any response, they stop. Second, you can think of a funny line that will show you are **comfortable** with your friendship and what they think doesn't bother you. Or third, you can ask them to **stop** teasing or bring in another friend or adult to help you. Often creating a scene by yelling, crying, or retaliating adds fuel to the fire and keeps the teasing going.

I have a best friend that is a boy, but I want a best friend that is a girl, but I can't seem to have a friend that likes me at all.

Finding a friend that likes you often starts with being a friend to someone first. *That can be kind of scary*—especially if you are uncertain if the person will like you at all. Being a friend means spending time together and sharing experiences. A fun place to start looking for a friend is while you're doing *something that you like to do*—you will find someone who also enjoys that same thing. If you like to sing, maybe you could find someone in music class or in a choir who wants to sing after school. Or if you like chess, maybe you could join the chess club to find someone who likes it as well. Friends often discover they have similar interests, and their friendship develops from time spent together doing those things. There will almost always be times in your life where finding friends is challenging—changing schools, moving, or having a friend move away are all times when you will need to have patience as you meet new people.

. . . .

I have a CRUSH, and a BIG one! Is this OK, and how can I deal?

A crush usually means you are interested in someone in a bigger way than you are with other friends. Maybe you notice them more than you notice other people, and you'd like to be closer or spend more time with them. Having stronger feelings for people is *a natural part of growing up*. If you find that thinking about your crush is keeping you from talking to or being with other friends, then the crush is getting in the way. Finding safe places to get to know your crush, like at school or in a club, is a great way to build your friendship. When a relationship moves from a crush to a trusted friendship, and when you are ready and it feels safe, you can share your feelings with the person. But if you have an idea that the other

person would not understand or that you are not ready, it is also okay to let the *exciting feelings* of liking someone stay private and not act on them.

. . . .

Why do we "like" boys when we're 11 but not 6? When should you begin to "like" boys? Confused!

Sometimes it seems like *all of a sudden* liking boys is all other girls can talk about. You may not have the same feelings because you have other things on your mind—that can be confusing! As you get older, you may find your feelings changing *from confused to interested*. It is pretty common when people are in puberty to start to be attracted to each other in new ways, but it actually doesn't happen in a single moment—*it occurs over time*. And there is no specific age when those feelings should start. You may find that liking someone means also having sexual feelings for them, which is entirely normal—another human experience.

. . . .

Do boys have crushes on us or is it just a rumor?

All girls (and guys!) have attractions to people. Liking someone, caring about someone, appreciating someone—these are all terrific things that humans get to experience with each other. Sometimes these feelings lead to relationships or friendships, but they certainly don't have to. Your feelings are yours. And it's likely that as you grow up, you will like *lots* of people, and lots of people will like you, because there are lots of likable people! Sometimes you will *like* that you like someone, and sometimes liking someone might not feel so comfortable. Part of growing up is learning how to be in healthy relationships. (If you are interested in learning more about questions boys have about girls, flip this book over to Chapter 12 on the boys' side and *read all about it!*)

What is "gay"?

Being gay, or *homosexual*, means being primarily attracted to other people of the SAME SEX for sexual partnerships. As you are growing up and exploring relationships and attractions, you will experience many feelings *for a wide range of people*. Most of the people in the world are heterosexual—which means they are primarily attracted to people of the opposite sex for sexual relationships. However, throughout history there have always been some people who are ATTRACTED to their same gender. *Time and experiences* in all sorts of friendships and relationships help you DISCOVER and UNDERSTAND your sexuality. (Read on for more questions and answers about being gay, and flip the book over to pages 61–63 on the boys' side for more information that is helpful for both girls and boys.)

· ·

What is the right grade to start dating?

Dating is one of the experiences *couples choose* so that they can spend time together to EXPLORE their relationship. There are all sorts of "dates"—watching a movie, eating at a restaurant, going on a bike ride, or even just hanging out. Sometimes dating means just two people alone, and sometimes it means you are in a crowd or with a group. The whole idea of a date is to GET TO KNOW each other better. Some families and cultures have a specific age in mind when they think dating is "right" because they see it as a step toward a more serious relationship, and they want to make certain you are SAFE and PREPARED. You may have a different idea of what a "date" means than your family does. So a good way to look for answers would be to have a CONVERSATION with your family *where everyone can share their ideas*. As difficult as it is to see at times— especially when there are different ideas—parents are invested and interested in knowing who you are with, where you are going, and what your plans are so they can help you to be safe and to have fun.

11. How Can I Make My Mom Seem Like More of an Option to Talk To?

. . . And Other Questions About Your Relationship with Your Parents

What if you like a boy but you don't know how to break it to mom that her baby girl LIKES SOMEONE?

Talking with parents about friendships and relationships can sometimes be challenging for a lot of reasons. Parents might be surprised by what you have to say, might change their opinions about you or your friend, or might have advice that you weren't looking for. "Liking" someone means you have feelings for the person that seem different than feelings you have for other friends—that you are interested in that person in a new or bigger way than you used to be. You might worry that your mom might not think you are old enough to *like* someone, and that she will be concerned or surprised. It might help to start off the conversation with something like, "Mom, some of my feelings are changing about people. I think I like someone in my class and *I would like to tell you about it* but I am worried what you will say or think."

I feel weird when my mom talks to me and it seems like we are **FIGHTING ALL THE TIME.** I just think she doesn't understand. She thinks I don't understand. It's, well, it's majorly weird! What do I do?

Living with your family gives you an important place to learn skills that you'll use *throughout the rest of your life*. However, it isn't always easy for parents and kids to get along. Sometimes there are topics or emotions that are uncomfortable and difficult. Maybe you feel like your mom gives you too much advice or that her ideas don't feel realistic. Maybe you think she is critical, or you argue more than anything else. It might be helpful to just *talk about talking* with your mom. Try to find a time to connect when there isn't something to argue about. You could start with, "It always seems like we are arguing—it would be nice to talk things over without yelling at each other." Let her know how you are feeling—*most likely she is hoping for some changes as well*. If you find you are always fighting, learning how to take a break and come back together when you both calm down can be key. Families who are struggling may need to call upon resources like counselors to help them work on ways to improve their communication.

How can I make MY MOM seem like more of an option to talk to?

Sometimes it's challenging to bring up certain topics with your family. That might be because your parents don't have any practice talking about certain topics, which makes them feel as uncomfortable as you do. Maybe you feel like your parents don't "hear" what you are trying to say. Or maybe just finding a time to talk is half the challenge—parents can be distracted by lots of responsibilities, so you need to invite them into the conversation. You might try saying something like, "Hey, mom—*I would love to talk through something* that is going on with my

friends. Would you have some time after dinner?" Or, "Mom, want to walk the dog together tonight? I have something on my mind." Sometimes its easier to start the conversation by writing her a note.

. . . .

My mom doesn't like to see me growing up, so I don't know how she will accept that I am growing up. How can I show her kindly that I'm NOT A BABY anymore?

Sometimes our bodies and our brains *change so fast* that our parents can't keep track. And sometimes we feel ready to have new responsibilities, but our parents are less certain. Every family makes adjustments as each person grows up, and part of the process is *negotiating decisions within a family*. Sometimes a decision in a family belongs just to the adults, sometimes it can belong to the kids, and sometimes it can be shared. Have a conversation with your family to tell them what you are thinking and experiencing if you feel ready to make your own decision but they are less certain. Everyone has the courage for even a one-minute conversation—it's a place to start.

. . . .

Should my dad know I am going through puberty?

Dads are invested in their daughters' lives in puberty *and beyond!* Some dads may not have much experience talking about girls' body changes since they have only been through their own puberty experience, so you may need to *help your dad understand* through your own stories or words about what puberty is like for a girl. Dads can be amazing advocates—they want the puberty experience to go well for their daughters. Sharing your *thoughts and feelings* with your dad helps him to discover some of the ways you are growing up.

Why do teens start to HATE their parents?

Becoming a teenager does *not* mean you will automatically hate your parents. In fact, most teens say that their parents are the *most important people in their lives*. As we get older, we begin to develop our own ideas and opinions, and sometimes those ideas are different from our parents' ideas, which creates conflict. As we work through our conflicts with our families, it's important to take a break from the conversation when it gets too heated, coming back to it when we can be calmer. It's also important to look for things that we can agree on and to make compromises when we can't agree. *Living with your family helps you* to learn about how to get along with others, how to love others, how to be challenged, and how to grow.

. . . .

Why do I LOVE MY FAMILY so much?

Your family gives you a safe place where you are *accepted and loved*. Families encourage us when we need support and they show us how to forgive when a mistake has been made. *It's no wonder you love your family!*

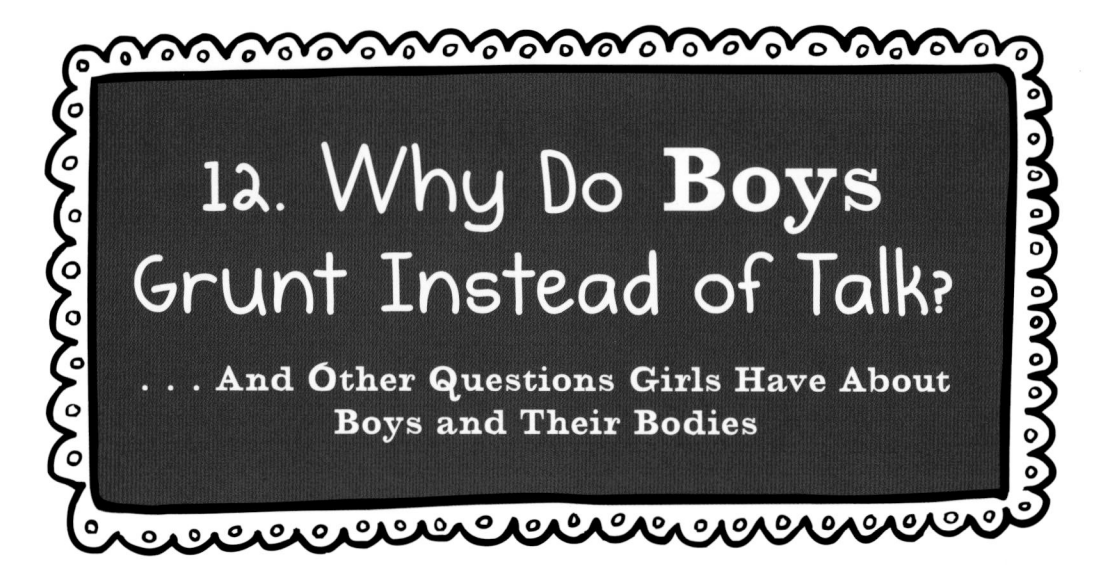

12. Why Do **Boys** Grunt Instead of Talk?

. . . And Other Questions Girls Have About Boys and Their Bodies

Do girls have totally different FEELINGS than boys?

Boys have the **same emotions** as girls—sad, mad, happy, jealous, disappointed, etc. But *the same experience* may draw out a **different** response in a boy than it does in you. It may sometimes seem like boys feel less sad or scared—maybe a boy tells a joke and laughs at a sad moment in a movie or responds in some other way that doesn't seem to match your own feelings at the time. However, it is important to recognize that *boys have feelings too*. Sometimes in our **culture** boys aren't given the same **permission** to show and share their emotions as girls. *Can you imagine how hard that would be?*

. . . .

Do boys feel as awkward as girls do about puberty?

Boys **worry** over a lot of the same things that girls do about puberty. Will someone notice I have pimples? Am I the right size? Am I **normal?** Will the person I like like me back? Because puberty is a *human experience*, everyone has some of the **same concerns**.

Why do boys grunt instead of talk?

Sometimes it seems like *boys use fewer words than girls*. Generally, girls' language skills—their ability to use words to express themselves—develops in their brains earlier than in boys' brains. Sometimes girls are more talkative because they have more practice using words. Sometimes girls need to *leave space* in the conversation by pausing, so boys can add their ideas.

. . . .

Why do boys have bigger arm muscles? It's not fair!

Both boys and girls develop stronger and bigger muscles as they go through puberty. However, you are right, boys will typically get broader shoulders and bigger arms than girls. Testosterone is the primary hormone that changes a boy's body during puberty. And even though girls also have a small amount of testosterone (in addition to their primary hormones called estrogen and progesterone) boys' *significant testosterone level* helps create muscle definition and larger muscles.

. . . .

My question is why do the boys' penises GO UP? Why can't they just stay down?

Girls have *three* openings between their legs: a urethra that connects to the bladder, a vagina that leads to the uterus, and an anus that is at the end of the intestines and the digestive system. All three openings have their own unique functions. A boy has *two* openings: a urethra in the penis that is shared between his bladder and his testicles, and an anus that connects to his digestive system. So, a penis has two jobs to do. Its regular job is being available to pee, and its new job that starts during puberty is to release sperm. To do its new job, a penis changes its shape in order to keep the urethra from getting mixed up in its work! In order to release sperm, a penis will change from *relaxed* to *straight and erect*. After the work of

releasing sperm, it goes back to relaxed so that it can be available to release urine. (Is it hard to picture all of this? Check out the illustrations on page 37 on the boys' side to put it all together.)

When a boy's penis goes up DOES IT SHOOT UP or does it slowly lift up?

A penis gets erect when *blood fills up the vessels in the penis*. It can happen when a boy is expecting it to go erect, or when it is inconvenient, like while a boy is giving a speech in front of the class. A penis usually goes erect over seconds, not minutes.

Does the penis GET STIFF just over night? When it does get stiff, DOES IT HURT?

A penis can become erect (or stiff) during the day and during the night. *It does not hurt for the penis to be erect.* (More interesting facts about penises can be found in Chapter 9 on the boys' side.)

So, at what age can a boy have an erection? Age 8? Age 12? Age 39? What age?

A boy's penis is able to go erect *even before he is born*. Sometimes when a baby boy gets his diaper changed, his penis goes erect. However, it is not until puberty that sperm is available in the testicles to be released.

Why do boys' penises hurt when you step on them?

Throughout our bodies we have networks of **nerves** that alert our brains to pain or touch or tickling. In boys' and girls' bodies, many nerve cells surround the outside parts of our **reproductive organs**—like a boy's penis and testicles or a girl's clitoris (a particularly small and sensitive spot just above a girl's urethra and vagina). These areas are very **sensitive** to touch and to pain.

. . . .

When boys have SPERM is it like how girls have a period and they have to wear pads and tampons? Can boys control their "period thing"?

Boys do not have periods like girls. A girl releases a single egg one at a time and has a period over four to seven days, while a boy releases hundreds of millions of sperm in a **single moment**—more like a sneeze than a period. These many millions of sperm are released from the tip of the penis in about a teaspoon of white, cloudy fluid called **semen**. When a boy releases sperm, it is called **ejaculation**. Girls have a period about once a month *no matter what they think or do*, and boys can **release** sperm any time on any day. Since a penis generally needs to be touched to release semen, it rarely happens as a big surprise in the middle of math class, so boys do not wear anything to protect their clothing like girls do.

. . . .

Do sperms have brains?

No, sperm do not have brains. *Penises don't know how* to make decisions on their own either. Only the **person** with the penis and the sperm has a brain.

Where does sperm go during the day?

Millions and millions of sperm **hang out** during the day and the night in the testicles where they are produced until the moment they are released, which is called **ejaculation**.

. . . .

If you are Joe's best friend, and you know that he is having an ERECTION, and he doesn't know, should you tell him or not?

Joe knows. A boy can **feel** when he has an erection without even looking down to see if he does or not.

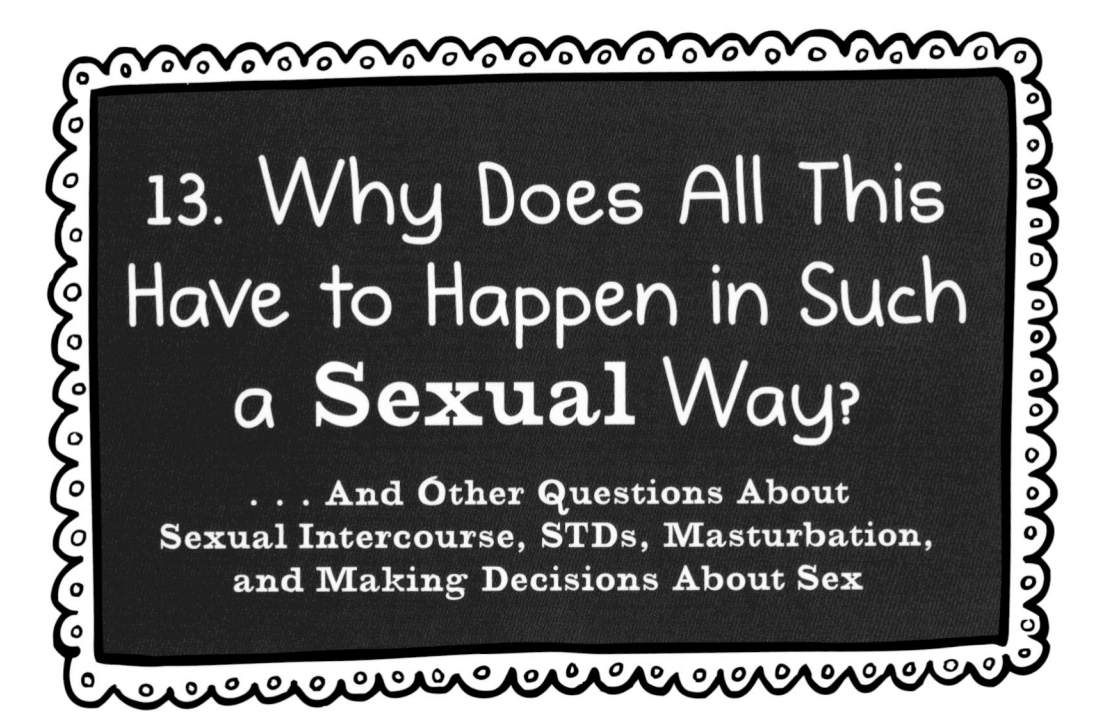

13. Why Does All This Have to Happen in Such a **Sexual** Way?

. . . And Other Questions About Sexual Intercourse, STDs, Masturbation, and Making Decisions About Sex

Do people have to plan or do something special to bring eggs and sperm together?

An egg inside a woman's body can't just wake up one day and decide to become a baby. *Two people need to make a decision together* to bring their bodies so close that a man's erect penis can go inside a woman's vagina. The penis then releases *hundreds of millions* of sperm in the vagina. Those millions of sperm swim through the cervix into the uterus and even up into the fallopian tubes. When there is an egg present, it takes only one tiny microscopic sperm to fertilize the egg—a single sperm actually enters the egg and then the egg shuts down to all the other sperm, becoming a brand-new cell. The brand-new cell is called a zygote. Then, the zygote starts to divide and divide and divide into more and more cells. The dividing group of cells travels down the fallopian tubes and plants itself on the lining of the uterus, where it continues to divide and grow. Eventually, it becomes a baby. Wild, isn't it? All of us started off as a *single tiny microscopic cell!*

How do the boys' and the girls' parts fit so perfectly together? Is it planned that way?

It *is* pretty amazing to think about . . . and kind of mysterious and sometimes challenging to picture. You are not the first person to shake her head at the whole idea! When a man and a woman bring their bodies so close together that a man's erect penis fits inside the woman's vagina, we call that sexual intercourse. Some people shorten the words to having sex, and some people honor the action by saying words like making love. Whichever words you use, sexual intercourse involves two people making a decision *together* to bring their bodies *together* when the egg and sperm can come *together*. It's a lot of together!

When do you know when you are READY to have sex?

Being "ready" generally means that both individuals that are thinking about having sexual intercourse are also thinking through what having sex will mean to them, both as individuals and as a couple. *Having sexual intercourse*—bringing two bodies so close together that they actually fit together—is one of the biggest actions possible for human beings. Some people and families believe sexual intercourse belongs only in committed adult relationships where both people have the maturity to be ready, such as in a marriage.

Do people have sex regularly?

Choosing to have sex is dependent on many things—having the ability to have sex, having someone who also wants to have sex with you at that time, and being together with that person *in a safe place*. Some people never have sex, some have sex a few times in their lives, and some people have sex often.

Around what age do most people START having sex for life?

There is *no exact age* for people to start having sex for life. Being "ready" can mean that you feel emotionally **prepared** to show and **share** your love with someone. Being ready can mean that you are physically ready to have sex. Being ready can mean that you are equipped to manage and understand the potential **consequences** of having sex, like a pregnancy or a sexually transmitted disease. Being ready can mean being married or in a committed relationship. Being ready can mean being an adult. Being ready *often* means all of the above. And sometimes people have sex and then don't for a while.

. . . .

Where is the most likely place to have sex?

Most people choose a **private** and **comfortable** place to have sex where both people can concentrate on each other and not be interrupted.

. . . .

Is it nice to have sex? Is it uncomfortable or comfortable?

People choose to have sex because it can be a **feel-good** experience both *physically and emotionally*. However, it's possible to have moments where it is less comfortable. Perhaps you are not in a comfortable location, perhaps you are **uncomfortable** about your feelings, or perhaps you are in an uncomfortable position with your bodies. When people who **love and respect** each other are uncomfortable in any way when having sex, then they should feel safe to talk it over and make adjustments to bring more comfort.

Can two humans do sex ANYtime? Or is it a time in the year the penis comes up?

Unlike some animals that have mating seasons, where the males and females have intercourse at a particular time of the year, there is *no special season* for two people to have sexual intercourse. A penis can come up (be erect) any time of the day or night, and two people can decide together to have sexual intercourse at any time of the year.

How long does it take to have sex?
Can you have sex for longer?

The act of **sexual intercourse**—when a penis goes inside a vagina—takes minutes, not hours or days. However, being **close** to someone and *showing and sharing your love* in anticipation of sexual intercourse or following sexual intercourse can add to that total time.

. . . .

Does having sex hurt? On a scale of 1-10 what number?

Having sex means bringing two bodies *very close together*. It is possible—just like when we hug someone or shake hands—that, either intentionally or unintentionally, we might hurt someone. People generally **choose** to have sex because it brings **pleasure** to both people and it communicates **love** and commitment. If it hurts for any reason, then the person that feels pain can speak up to ask for something to change. Earlier, we talked about how our bodies have nerves that communicate to our brains about touch or pain or tickling. There are lots of places on our bodies that have *an abundance of nerves*, so that when touched, they feel especially nice. Boys' penises and testicles and girls' vaginas and clitorises are places that have an abundance of nerves that make them very **sensitive** to touch. When people respect and care for each other while having sex, it can feel very good. When a boy's penis releases sperm, it is called ejaculation, and it creates a sensation all over his body, called an orgasm, that is very **satisfying**. *Girls have orgasms too*, when their whole bodies are excited sexually and the muscles in their vaginas and uteruses contract. **It feels good**, but it has nothing to do with releasing an egg.

What is MASTURBATION about then?

Masturbation is when someone **touches** their own body parts to create sexual feelings. For boys, that often means touching their own penises, and for girls it often means rubbing their vulvas and clitorises. There are many people who **masturbate** and many people who do not—boys and girls, young and old—all over the world and across history. It is a **choice** whether someone masturbates, and they generally choose it *because it feels good*. Sometimes people worry that masturbating will make them less healthy or make them act funny, but scientists and doctors have never found any truth to these worries. Masturbation can be a **safe** and **normal** choice for people when it's done in **private** and in balance with all the other activities in someone's life—like playing sports and doing homework! (There is more information about masturbation for both guys *and* girls on the boys' side of the book on page 41–42.)

· ·

Is it okay to be SCARED to have sex?

Deciding to have sex is *a big decision*—sex is one of the biggest actions possible between two people. That is why treating the decision with **respect** and honoring your **feelings** is important. It is not unusual to be nervous or scared to have sex—it can be a sign that you are aware of the potential risks and consequences. When both people see themselves as ready to make the decision to have sex, when they feel they are in a **relationship** of love and respect and commitment, they may feel less scared. Some people wait until they are more grown-up and can manage the relationship and the **consequences** of having sex. Because sex is one of the biggest human actions, it should be no surprise that you can have some of the biggest human consequences as a result of having sex. What are some of these? Well, *having a baby* is an amazingly huge consequence. And another big consequence is sharing a disease—*a sexually transmitted disease*. We are going to have more conversations about both—just keep reading!

How can I do "it" without getting embarrassed? How do I ask someone to do "it"? It = sex.

When two people are in a relationship, they make all sorts of decisions together—like what movie they want to see, or whether to arrive early to the basketball game or leave at halftime. Decisions between two people require understanding, negotiation, listening, and talking. The same communication is needed between two people when they are making decisions about sex. It's helpful to pay attention to your feelings as you make decisions. Sometimes being embarrassed is a sign that you are not yet comfortable with your decision. There are *millions and millions* of things two people can do together before they even think about having sex—holding hands, walking the dog, kissing, going to the park, having dinner together, talking on the phone, debating, arguing, and laughing are just a few. *Most relationships* don't end up including sexual intercourse. Asking someone to do "it" typically means a relationship has had time to experience many other decisions and events so that sex feels like a natural progression—not a surprise question and not a choice made under pressure.

· ·

Why can't a woman grow sperm and an egg so they don't have to have sex?

Part of what makes us interesting and different from one another is that we have messages from *two different birth parents* that get brought together when an egg and sperm meet. Our sizes, hair colors, and even parts of our personalities are determined by heredity. If we each just had one birth parent contributing both cells, we would all be clones from generation to generation. Besides, families also *become more interesting* as we bring two different ones together when a baby is born.

Why do people have sex? It's so gross!

It's easy to think that having sex is gross *since it is hard to picture*, involves body parts that you normally don't show others, and involves feelings you have yet to experience. As your body and brain mature, you'll learn more about sex and have more sexual feelings. Those feelings and experiences will help you to have a better understanding of sex.

. . . .

Why does everyone think sexual intercourse is so gross except the people who are doing it?

Although our brains *are wired to be sexual* from the time we are born, it takes having experiences in relationships to help us understand how to interpret sexual feelings and make decisions about sex. People who wait to have sex until they have the information they need and the right person and relationship to share the experience with are more likely to enjoy having sex.

. . . .

Why does sex have such a bad reputation then?

Because it is mysterious, important, and a little scary, people sometimes talk about sex in a fearful way. *The consequences of sex can be life changing*, difficult, or dangerous—like having a baby or getting a disease—so people don't want others to jump into having sex before they understand those *big* things.

. . . .

That's weird how sex works. Do you have to do it?

No one ever has to have sex. *It is always your choice.*

Why do people talk about sex in songs? Like in rap.

People talk about sex in songs because sex is mysterious, interesting, passionate, challenging, and part of many relationships. People use songs *to process their thinking* about things and to tell their stories. Some songs glorify sex and some songs diminish sex and make it ugly. Some people make their songs sexual to make them more exciting so that people will buy their music.

. . . .

What is rape?

Rape is when someone takes away someone else's choice about having sex. It is illegal for someone to take away your decision to have sex—the decision to have sex belongs to *both* people, not just one person. It is important to speak to a trusted adult resource if you think that someone you know has had sex without consenting. Sometimes when someone has been raped, the victim feels like it was her fault or she feels embarrassed, shy, ashamed, or afraid, which makes it hard to speak to someone about it. There are many experts who have ways to *support and help* someone who has been raped.

. . . .

Why, when people have sex, do they say they do more than what you told us about? Is it true that they do more?

Sexual intercourse is most often described as bringing two bodies together so that a penis enters a vagina. However, "*sex*" can mean other behaviors for sure—oftentimes people kiss, hold each other, and touch each other on other body parts as well.

Does KISSING have anything to do with sex?

Many people kiss while having sex, but two people can kiss without ever having sex, and it is possible to have sex without kissing.

. . . .

When people have sex, why do they breathe funny?

Just like *exercise*, the action of bringing two bodies together while having sex takes energy. It can also be very exciting, which can change someone's breathing so that it sounds deeper or more rapid.

. . . .

Does every penis fit in the vagina they want it to fit in?

Remember, a penis doesn't get to make any decisions on its own—it requires the guy attached to the penis along with the girl attached to the vagina to make a decision about sex. But most penises and vaginas fit together well.

. . . .

When you have sex, do you have to wait for the boy to be erected, or does he do it on command?

A penis needs to be erect to be firm enough to enter a vagina. A boy cannot tell his penis to become erect. Generally, a penis will go erect with touch or with the *idea of it being touched*.

Do you know when you are having sexual intercourse?

The action of *bringing bodies together* so that a penis enters a vagina is a big deal. Your two bodies are so close that you are skin-to-skin, and you can feel the penis come inside, so *you will know when it happens*. Both people get to be a part of the decision to have sexual intercourse.

· ·

Why does all this have to happen in such a SEXUAL WAY?

Being sexual is *part of being a* human being. Along with being sexual, we are also compassionate, curious, invested, competitive, emotional, and resilient. Sexuality is woven through who we are and is *wired into our brains*.

· ·

Can GAY PEOPLE have sex?

Yes. "Having sex" has many definitions. One is when a penis enters a vagina. But having sex also means when two people bring their bodies together in a sexual way. When two people of the same sex bring their bodies together to *show and share their love physically*, that is also called having sex.

· ·

How do people in wheelchairs have sex?

Whether or not the mechanics are the same, people in wheelchairs can *show and share their love* in many of the same ways that people who are not in wheelchairs do. They find a safe and private place, and they touch, kiss, and talk to their partners.

I just want to know, do people talk about having sex and then go get undressed and do it?

Usually making the decision to have sex means *more than* just talking, undressing, and doing. Some people also like to have a ROMANTIC dinner before sex, listen to music, or HOLD AND KISS each other in addition to having sex. Part of a sexual EXPERIENCE with someone can also mean *spending time together* in other ways in a safe and COMFORTABLE place.

. . . .

DID MY PARENTS REALLY DO THAT?
How do I learn to handle that thought?

Because HAVING SEX is generally an act people do in PRIVATE while they are at least partially naked, it can be wild to imagine people that you know having sex! *It can be especially challenging* when you are just getting used to the whole concept of sex in the first place. *Generally*, over time as you grow in your understanding of how sexual behavior fits into people's lives *and* you do more and more thinking about your own experiences and relationships, thinking about your parents becomes less consuming.

. . . .

Who thought of having sexual intercourse in the first place and how did they think of THAT?

Great question! From the beginning of LIFE ON EARTH, many plants and most animals have REPRODUCED by fertilizing seeds and cells *to ensure their survival.* Since our *brains are wired* to be sexual, perhaps early humans acted from INSTINCT or learned about sex from watching other species.

Why are parents SO UNCOMFORTABLE talking about sexual intercourse?

There are *a lot of reasons* parents might feel uncomfortable talking about sexual intercourse. Having sex is private, intimate, and *usually not something people talk about every day*, so sometimes people have a hard time talking out loud about it. Sometimes parents are nervous that they will be embarrassed or say the wrong thing. A lot of parents did not have conversations with their own parents about sex, so they don't know about the ways parents and kids can talk about it. Some parents wonder if kids are too young to talk about sex because they believe sex is only for adults. Although parents want kids to know about the consequences of sex, sometimes they feel *scared* or *too frightened to speak up*. And sometimes parents just feel overwhelmed by the enormity of the subject—from the mechanics to the consequences, *sex is a big topic!*

. . . .

What are some sexually translated diseases?

Actually, they are called sexually transmitted diseases (STDs), and there are *more than thirty different* STDs that both girls and boys can get if they are exposed to them. All of these diseases have similarities and differences. What makes them the same is that they occur from sharing body fluids (like semen and vaginal fluids) during sexual contact. What makes them different from one another is how they show up in our bodies and how we treat them. You cannot tell someone has an STD by looking at them, and it is important for both girls and guys to know how to protect themselves from STDs. (There is more information about sexually transmitted diseases for both guys *and* girls on the boys' side of the book on pages 80–83.)

14. Are Hips for Babies to Rest On?

. . . And Other Questions About Pregnancy, Pregnancy Prevention, Childbirth, and Babies

How long does it take for the SPERM to meet the EGG?

When sperm are **released** into the vagina, they use their tails to swim and move around the vagina into the uterus and even up into the fallopian tubes. *Sperm can live for days* swimming around. If there is an egg present, as soon as a **single sperm** enters it, the egg is unavailable to the other hundreds of millions of sperm. How long it takes for a single **microscopic** sperm to find a single microscopic egg depends on how fast the sperm swims and where the egg is located—it could take *something like hours*. Eggs are fertilized on their way from the ovaries to the uterus in the fallopian tubes.

. . . .

Can you make a baby any old time?

People can have sexual intercourse any old time of the day or night; however, there needs to be an **egg** present for a **baby** to be conceived, and there is *not always* an egg present outside of an ovary. If someone doesn't want to get pregnant, they should always use **contraception**.

I read in a book that if you have sex standing up you don't get pregnant. Is that true?

Women can get pregnant standing, sitting, or lying down. Women can get pregnant having sex in a bed, in a car, or on a couch. Women can get pregnant if a penis and a vagina are *close enough to touch*.

. . . .

Can you get pregnant other ways besides sexual intercourse? (I've heard sitting on a toilet seat?)

You *cannot* get pregnant from sitting on a toilet seat, touching a doorknob, shaking hands, or kissing. *You cannot get pregnant unless* a penis gets close to a vagina. Sometimes there is sperm present in fluid on the tip of a penis, and if that touches a woman's vulva *even for a second*, it's possible that sperm would use the fluid available in the vagina to swim inside the woman.

. . . .

If a man wears a CONDOM so he can have sexual intercourse, what's the point of putting the penis inside the vagina because it can't do anything?

Just because a penis has a condom on it doesn't mean that it can't do anything. Even though a condom will help prevent sperm from going into the vagina and reduce the risk of sharing a sexually transmitted disease, it still allows a guy to ejaculate sperm, and the resulting orgasm is very pleasurable.

. . . .

Where do you get condoms?

Grocery stores and drugstores are typical places people buy condoms.

Why do people continue to have sex once they've had a baby and don't want any more babies?

People continue to have sex because it **feels good** and it's a way to feel **connected** with their partner—having sex is a way to *show and share your love.* If people do not want to have a baby but do want to have sex, then they need to take responsibility to protect their bodies so they can reduce the chance of an egg and sperm coming together. We call that protection **birth control** or **contraception**. There are several ways that people use birth control—one is to not have sex when there is an egg present. Another choice is for a man to wear a covering over his penis called a **condom** that keeps the sperm inside after it has been released. There are also coverings for a woman's cervix that will keep sperm from entering the uterus. It is also possible for a woman to take additional hormones in the form of a pill, shot, or device inserted under her skin that tells her body *not to release an egg.* There are all sorts of *traditions and beliefs* in cultures and faith groups about contraception. What is essential to know is that if people are having sexual intercourse, there is always a chance of getting pregnant.

. . . .

Is it true that if you have sex standing up you will get a baby boy?

Having a boy or having a girl is primarily related to **which sperm** finds the egg. We know from scientists who have looked at sperm very closely with special microscopes that there are different genetic messages in sperm. Scientists call some sperm "X," some sperm "Y," and all eggs "X." When an "X" sperm finds an egg, then the baby will be a **girl**. When a "Y" sperm finds an egg, the baby will be a **boy**. Some people try to work out how to increase the chances of having a boy or girl by giving people ideas about how and when to have sex. There is *no specific idea* that works every time.

Why wouldn't somebody want to have a baby if it's called a miracle?

Getting pregnant and having a baby means a *lot* of love, responsibility, diapers, crying, expense, time, attention, fun, and worry. There is a *lot* to celebrate when someone has a baby. Babies are amazing, lovable, and endearing—however, they require *twenty-four-hour attention and care*. When people have children but can't care for them because of illness, homelessness, or lack of resources, then some parents feel overwhelmed by how to give the love and attention that a child needs.

. . . .

How can a WHOLE NEW LIFE be born in only 9 months?

Isn't it amazing? All of the complex parts of a baby—seeing eyes, beating hearts, filtering livers, wiggling toes—start with two microscopic cells. Those cells come together to make a brand-new single cell, and from that single zygote comes the extraordinary you! By the way, while it takes a human baby nine months to grow, it takes an elephant baby two years, and a rabbit baby four weeks.

. . . .

Why can't boys have babies?

Men *do* have babies—all the time. Their part in having a baby is to contribute the sperm that provides half of the genetic makeup. The *physical act of carrying a baby* for forty weeks in a uterus and delivering the baby is ultimately a female's work because we have the body parts that are perfectly suited for that job. But a man can be supportive, encouraging, and helpful during pregnancy and childbirth, and do lots of work in caring for the baby after it is born.

How does the belly button relate to this?

An **umbilical cord** connects the baby from its abdomen to the mom's uterus during pregnancy. Made out of a combination of a vein and two arteries, it makes it possible for the *mother's and the baby's blood* to be **shared**. Every time a pregnant mom takes a breath, oxygen enters her lungs and travels through her body and the umbilical cord so that the baby's body gets the **oxygen** it needs. Every time the mom takes a bite of a sandwich, that sandwich is digested and all the vitamins, protein, calcium, and other **important nutrients** travel through her blood and through the umbilical cord so that the baby shares these nourishing things. *When a baby is born,* so is the cord. People assisting in the birth of the baby clamp and cut the cord once the baby is born. The inch or so of cord that remains on the baby dries up and falls off in a few days. The spot *where the cord was originally connected* becomes a **belly button**.

. . . .

How come some belly buttons go in and some go out? (Mine goes in.)

Not all **belly buttons** are the same, just like not all feet or elbows are the same. *There is no particular reason* your belly button is a particular size or shape.

. . . .

If you have sex 10 times will you have 10 babies?

It is possible to have sex ten times and have ten babies, but those ten times would be spaced around each pregnancy—once a pregnancy starts, having sex doesn't start a new **pregnancy**. Because sperm don't find every egg—and because a woman typically releases a single egg only once a month and it's not always obvious when an egg is present—people *usually* need to have sex **more than** ten times to have ten babies.

If you have sex for a very long time will you have twins?

Twins, triplets, or other multiple births do not happen because of the length of time someone has sex. There are two common ways for twins to be conceived. One is when more than one egg is released from the ovaries, so that when millions of sperm are swimming toward the egg, *two* egg/sperm cell combinations are created. These twins are called fraternal twins, and they can be two boys, two girls, or a girl and a boy, but they do not look exactly alike because they have two different sets of genetic material. *The second possibility* is that an egg and sperm come together to form a zygote, and then the zygote splits into two groups of cells. Because these two new groups of cells originally came from the same egg/sperm combination and share the exact genetic material, these identical twins can only be two girls or two boys, and they will be exactly the same in appearance. *Triplets, quadruplets, and so on* are often fraternal.

· ·

Could I have 3 babies at one time? P.S. Just say yes or no.

Yes.

· ·

Is a baby the funnest thing about having sex?

There are a lot of people who have sex who do not have a baby and call sex fun. In fact, generally people who are having sex have sex many more times than they have babies. Having a baby *is* fun. And having sex is fun too.

Is the pregnancy procedure uncomfortable?

Throughout her pregnancy, a woman might feel excited, nervous, uncomfortable, tired, and energized—*a whole range of feelings*. When pregnancy feels uncomfortable, a woman might be nauseated, feel pressure on her bladder that makes her need to pee, or have **challenges** digesting her food. *As a baby continues to develop and get bigger*, it will move, kick, and hiccup, which might feel painful or keep the pregnant mom from sleeping well.

. . . .

Do babies come out head first or feet first? Or does it really matter?

Babies *typically* turn upside down in the uterus a couple of weeks before they are ready to be born, then are born **head first** through the vagina. However, babies *can also be born* feet- or bottom- first. Some babies are born by cesarean section (or **C-section**). When this happens, a doctor makes a special cut or incision just above the mother's pubic bone through her belly and into her uterus, and the baby is born through that incision. Afterward, the mother's uterus and belly are stitched up by the surgeon.

. . . .

Is giving birth the most painful and joyful situation in life?

Yes, *for many women*, giving birth is both **painful** and **joyful**. The physical act of labor—the uterus contracting and pushing the baby through the vagina, or having the baby removed by cesarean section—requires the mother to manage her pain. The joyful part is finding out how much your body can do and *welcoming a beautiful baby* into the world.

Does it hurt when you have a baby? (Just wondering not worried.)

Yes, it does hurt. The uterus works very hard tensing and contracting to push the baby through the vagina. Giving birth also requires the mother to push down with a lot of energy so that she helps the baby *progress through the birth canal.* A mom giving birth often asks people to help her during labor, or strong contractions, by offering her encouraging words, touch, massage, sips of water, and other support. Moms may also ask to receive medicine that can help control the pain. Giving birth is a very powerful physical experience—like climbing a steep mountain—so the mom wants *resources and encouragement* throughout, and will also need time to rest and recover afterward.

. . . .

I was wondering if one ovary contained all girls, and the other all boys?

Nope. Both ovaries contain eggs that all have only an "X." It is the sperm that comes as an "X" or "Y" and determines if the baby will be a *girl or boy.*

. . . .

How the heck does the baby fit through the vagina?

Amazing, isn't it? A few things work together to help a baby fit through a vagina. First, a baby's skull is more flexible than an older child's. An infant's skull actually consists of several pieces, so that the bones can move together while the baby's head is in a tight space, and then the head expands again after the baby is born. Second, a vagina is quite flexible—it is both *elastic and muscular*—so it can stretch to accommodate a baby's head. And finally, a woman's hipbones loosen in their sockets to provide more flexibility for the baby to be born.

Some people are born with missing senses or qualities that make them DIFFERENT in some other unusual ways. Why is that?

There are many reasons a baby might be born with a physical challenge—from not having the ability to hear to having a foot that is differently shaped. Sometimes babies inherit conditions from their birth parents; sometimes something happens *as the cells divide* and work together to form different body parts. We don't always know the cause for some of the different ways that babies are born. Most people have something unique about their body that makes it different from others, like an unusual birthmark or the way an earlobe is shaped. Maybe you've noticed some of these *characteristics* with your own body.

. . . .

Are hips for babies to rest on?

Yes—*hips are wonderful places for babies to rest*. A woman's hips are also wider and more prominent than a man's. This means that when a woman is pregnant, her pelvis has the support it needs to hold the uterus as it gets bigger. Her wider hips also *allow the baby to fit through them* as it is being born.

. . . .

When you're pregnant, and your baby finally gets ears, can it hear you talking?

There are *tiny little bones* inside your ear canal. Once these are formed, these bones are able to conduct sound by vibrating against each other. Of course, babies can't tell us with words what they are hearing. However, some pregnant women can sense when a baby appears to move or calm itself *because of certain sounds*.

Are you ALWAYS HUNGRY when you're pregnant? I don't get it, because you give all of the food to the baby.

It is true that pregnant women need more *healthy food* and *calories* to take care of their **own bodies** *plus* their **growing babies**. In places where food is scarce, one of the biggest challenges in delivering healthy, full-size babies is making sure women have **enough to eat**.

. . . .

How do you find out that you are going to have a baby before your uterus gets big?

One of the ways that women notice that their bodies are **pregnant** is that they **stop having periods**. During the nine months a woman is pregnant, she does not have a period. Sometimes even before she notices her period has stopped, she experiences nausea or an upset stomach, or she notices that her nipples have darkened in color—*these are additional clues* she might be pregnant.

. . . .

At what age would it be possible to have a baby? Because I have seen movies about teenagers having babies. So I just wonder.

Once a girl begins to **release eggs** from her ovaries, it is possible for her to get **pregnant** if she has sexual contact with a boy where sperm from his penis can enter her vagina. A girl can assume that *once she is in puberty*, it's possible to get pregnant, since there are no flashing lights on our foreheads announcing, "Egg coming!"

Once the eggs come out, what if you do it again (you know, have sex), where do the new eggs come from? You've already used them. How do you get refills if you want another baby?

You are born with a **million** or so eggs in both ovaries, but *you do not continue to produce eggs* beyond that. You **release an egg** from that original supply of eggs once every period. So women that have more than one baby can have sex again, but they do not need to get "refills"—they release a new egg every month. Women release only a fraction of their eggs over a lifetime. Unused eggs just get *very* old and stay in the ovaries.

. . . .

Are there ways for a LESBIAN MOMS to have a baby?

Yes. Two lesbian moms (a gay couple of two women) can bring children into their lives through *adoption, foster parenting*, or using a *sperm donor* for conception.

. . . .

What about DONORS? I have a donor. They do things slightly a different way.

Most babies are **conceived** (when the egg and sperm come together) through sexual intercourse. There are also babies who are conceived *from an egg or sperm donated by someone*. **Artificial insemination** is when the cells are brought together in a laboratory by scientists and then *implanted as a group of cells* into a woman's uterus. It is also possible for donor sperm to be inserted into a woman's vagina to conceive with her egg in her own fallopian tube.

Why should my body go through puberty if I know I am going to adopt?

We don't have a switch anywhere to turn puberty off or on. And although you may choose to adopt when you are older, you may want some of the **other changes** of puberty to happen like *growing taller* or *getting breasts*.

. . . .

What if you do not want a little sister or brother but you get one?

Either way, you are a big sister and that is one of the **best jobs** in the world.

. . . .

What else is there I should know?

There are **so many things** to learn about our bodies as we grow older, it actually takes a **lifetime!** I think it is impossible to learn it all. At the same time, you now have learned most of the big ideas that are helpful to kids in puberty. I hope you will *continue to ask questions* and *seek information from important resources* as you grow up.

FLIP THIS BOOK TO READ THE BOYS' SIDE! ⤷